Sensational
Small Quilts

15 Projects from Wall Hangings to Throws

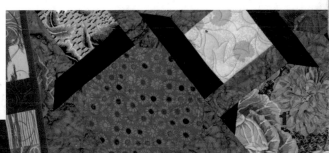

Edited by **Christine Doyle**

featuring **Darlene Zimmerman, Maggie Ball and Pam & Nicky Lintott**

kp

KRAUSE PUBLICATIONS
CINCINNATI, OHIO

www.fwmedia.com

media 14 13 12 11 10 5 4 3 2 1

DISTRIBUTED IN CANADA BY FRASER DIRECT
100 Armstrong Avenue
Georgetown, ON, Canada L7G 5S4
Tel: (905) 877-4411

DISTRIBUTED IN THE U.K. AND EUROPE BY F+W MEDIA INTERNATIONAL
Brunel House, Newton Abbot, Devon, TQ12 4PU, England
Tel: (+44) 1626 323200, Fax: (+44) 1626 323319
Email: postmaster@davidandcharles.co.uk

DISTRIBUTED IN AUSTRALIA BY CAPRICORN LINK
P.O. Box 704, S. Windsor NSW, 2756 Australia
Tel: (02) 4577-3555

Sensational small quilts : 15 projects from wall hangings to throws / edited by Christine Doyle.
p. cm.
Includes index.
ISBN-13: 978-1-4402-1441-7 (pbk. : alk. paper)
1. Quilts--Patterns. 2. Patchwork--Patterns. I. Doyle, Christine.
TT835.S4516 2010
746.46--dc22
2010027935

Edited by Christine Doyle and Kelly Biscopink
Designed by Steven Peters
Production coordinated by Greg Nock
Illustrations by Lindsay Quinter

METRIC CONVERSION CHART		
To convert	to	multiply by
Inches	Centimeters	2.54
Centimeters	Inches	0.4
Feet	Centimeters	30.5
Centimeters	Feet	0.03
Yards	Meters	0.9
Meters	Yards	1.1

THIS BOOK FEATURES PROJECTS FROM THESE GREAT F+W MEDIA, INC. TITLES:

Bargello Quilts with a Twist by Maggie Ball

Black & White and Pieced All Over by Kay M. Capps Cross

¡Caliente Quilts! by Priscilla Bianchi

Fat Quarter Fun by Karen Snyder

Granny Quilt Décor by Darlene Zimmerman

Granny Quilts by Darlene Zimmerman

Jelly Roll Quilts by Pam and Nicky Lintott

Layer Cake, Jelly Roll and Charm Quilts by Pam and Nicky Lintott

Log Cabin Quilts with Attitude by Sharon V. Rotz

Quilts from Lavender Hill Farm by Darlene Zimmerman

Rainy Day Appliqué by Ursula Michael

Scrap Quilt Sensation by Katharine Guerrier

Simple Stained Glass Quilts by Daphne Greig and Susan Purney Mark

Sugar Sack Quilts by Glenna Hailey

Traditional Quilts with a Twist by Maggie Ball

CONTENTS

INTRODUCTION

Small quilts are, for many quilters, the most exciting projects to begin. These quilts provide an opportunity to experiment with patterns, color combinations and fabric lines that we may be curious to try, but aren't ready to commit to in a full-size quilt. Small quilts are also the homemade items we give to those wo love as gifts for births, graduations, holidays and weddings. We hang small quilts on the walls, we drape them over cribs and rocking chairs, and we cover our family with them. And best of all, they're quick and easy to make!

The projects in Chapter 1 can help any quilter break free from a "quilting rut" and try something new. Gather inspiration from the patterns, the fabrics and the methods in these projects. Try making the quilts in this chapter, but put a piece of your own artistic aesthetic into them. Throw in your favorite zinger fabric, or incorporate your initials into the quilting to put your special stamp on the quilt. Use the black and white theme from Elegance (page 18) in the bargello blocks from Bainbridge Delft (page 26) with an appliquéd border from La Bohemia Wall Quilt (page 38). The sky is the limit!

In Chapter 2, you'll make beautiful quilts from the scraps you have been collecting for years. Every quilter saves scraps, planning to make a scrap quilt one day, but few ever get around to it. All of those little pieces, all of that sorting and fussy cutting begins to seem tedious and almost impossible. But you will have the small scrap quilts in this chapter whipped up in no time at all! You'll also learn some new patterns and techniques for making scrap quilts quick, easy and altogether fun. If you just can't bring yourself to make a true scrap quilt, these projects can be made with small amounts of fabric, including pre-cuts. Raid your stash for the perfect bits of fabric for these quilts.

Take the time in Chapter 3 to connect to your quilting heritage. If you've never made a traditional quilt, this may be a good time to try one. The beautiful intricacies of a traditional quilt are enjoyable to try in a small quilt, and the results are stunning. If you're not a fan of traditional quilts, consider making one of these projects in bright, modern fabrics to truly combine the old and the new.

Small projects give quilters the chance to experiment and try new things without committing to a long-term project or a large fabric requirement. Challenge yourself to make quilts you would never try before—you may discover a whole new style of quilting!

From Jelly Roll Quilts
by Pam and Nicky Lintott

GENERAL INSTRUCTIONS

written by Darlene Zimmerman

CHOOSING FABRIC

Publishing a book is a long process. If identical fabrics are no longer available, don't despair! Choose similar fabrics if you like the original quilt, or be daring and choose a different colorway for an interesting variation.

Whatever fabrics you choose, try to buy the best quality. Quality fabrics will be easier to sew and you will have a better finished product. The colors will last longer, and the fabric will hold up well to wear and tear.

PREPARING THE FABRIC

You may choose to prewash your fabric—or not. It is a personal decision. The fabric will lose some body and you may have some shrinking and raveling. You can restore the body with a little spray starch or fabric sizing, but don't leave such products in the finished quilt long-term; they may attract dirt and bugs.

You can test a fabric for color bleeding by spritzing a small area with water, then ironing it right sides together with a white fabric. If there is color transference, it would be safer to prewash.

Ironing the folds out of the fabric is a necessary step for accurate cutting.

CUTTING

Accuracy in cutting is important for the pieces to fit together properly in your quilt. Some tips for accurate cutting:

- Work in good light, daylight if possible.
- Iron the fabrics before cutting.
- Cut only two layers of fabric at a time. Any time saved in cutting more layers will be lost when trying to fit together the inaccurate pieces.
- Keep your tools from slipping. Use a film or sandpaper that adheres to the back of the tools.
- Use a sharp rotary cutter and a good mat. Mats and cutting blades do wear out over time, so replace them as needed.

USING THE TOOLS

For most of the projects in this book, you will need a self-healing mat, rotary cutter, various sizes of quilting rulers, a sewing machine, scissors, pins and other notions. These items are all easily found at your local craft retailers.

Use a rotary cutter only on a self-healing mat to avoid damage to your cutting surface. When cutting, push away from you with the blade—this will help minimize the potential for injury. When cutting a straight edge, slide the rotary cutter blade down the edge of an acrylic quilting ruler, being sure to keep your fingers out of the way.

Any additional tool requirements or suggestions are found in the project sections. A short tutorial on two of these tools is found on page 15.

SEWING

Quarter-inch seams are so important! If at all possible, find a quarter-inch foot for your machine, made specifically for quilt piecing. They are well worth the small investment.

If you have problems with the "mad feed dogs" chewing up your fabric, try these tricks to tame them:

- Insert a new needle, a sharps or quilting needle, an 80/12 would be a good size.
- Clean and oil your sewing machine, particularly under the throat plate.
- Chain-sew whenever possible.
- Begin and end with a scrap of fabric.

UNSEWING

It's a fact of life, mistakes happen. Use a seam ripper when necessary. Strive for perfection, learn from your mistakes, but also forgive yourself for not being perfect. The Amish place a deliberate mistake in a quilt as a "humility block" because they believe only God is perfect.

PRESSING

Remember the purpose of pressing is to make the seam, unit, block, and the quilt top as flat as possible. Iron from the right side whenever possible. Follow the pressing arrows given in the directions. If you follow these, most, if not all, of your seams will alternate.

TWISTING THE SEAM

Try this trick whenever you have any type of four-patch unit. It will make the center seam intersection lie flatter.

1 Before pressing the last seam on a four-patch, grasp the seam with both hands about an inch from the center seam. Twist in opposite directions, opening up a few threads in the seam (Figure 1).

2 Press one seam in one direction, and the other seam in the opposite direction. In the center you will see a tiny four-patch appear, and the center now lies very flat (Figure 2).

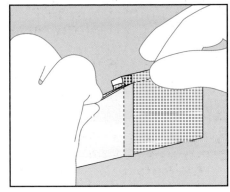

Figure 1

TRY THIS!

Try this quick check to see if you are sewing an exact ¼" seam allowance: Cut three 1½" x 3½" strips. Sew them together on the long edges. Press. The square should now measure 3½." If not, adjust your seam allowance. (Also check that you have pressed correctly.)

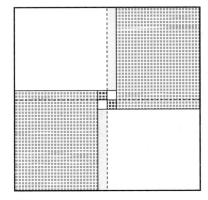

Figure 2

BORDERS

We often make adding borders to a quilt more difficult than it needs to be. Simply cut the strips designated for the borders and piece them as needed. Some people prefer to piece the borders on the diagonal, but the print can also be matched with a straight seam. Choose which method works best for your project.

Place the border strips on top of the quilt to measure the length or width of the quilt through the middle. Always measure with two border strips together so the borders are guaranteed to be the same length. Crease the border strips at the proper length, but cut an extra inch longer for leeway. Pin the borders to the quilt and sew.

BATTING

The type of batting you use is a personal choice. Cotton batting will give you a flat, traditional look and will shrink a bit when you wash the quilt, giving it a slightly puckered look. Cotton batting is more difficult to hand-quilt, but it will machine-quilt nicely, because the layers of the quilt will not shift readily.

Polyester batting has a bit more loft (puffiness) than a cotton batt and is easier to hand-quilt, but is more slippery, which can cause shifting when machine quilting. Combination poly-and-cotton battings can give you the best qualities of both and are a good choice for hand and machine quilting.

QUILTING

After you have finished your quilt top, it's time to consider quilting. Some tops need to be marked for quilting before they are basted, others while they are being quilted. Whichever device you use, pretest it on scraps of fabric from the project to see if it can be easily removed.

Create your "quilt sandwich" by layering the batting in between the quilt top and the backing fabric, and basting the layers together with safety pins or thread 4" apart. The batting and backing should be cut at least 4" larger than the quilt top.

Some of the quilts in this book were hand-quilted, others machine-quilted on a sewing machine, and still others sent out to a longarm quilter. Feel free to create your own quilting designs.

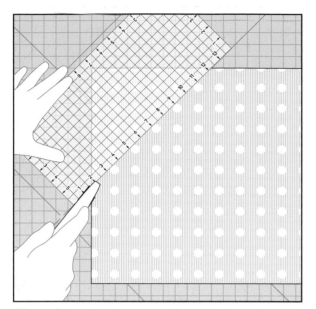

Figure 1

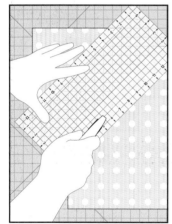

Figure 2a

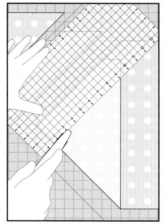

Figure 2b

BINDING

Generally, I use double bias or double straight-of-grain binding for any straight edges, and single, bias binding for curved edges.

1 To cut bias binding, trim off the selvages and trim both the bottom and top edges of the fabric chosen for the binding. Using the 45-degree line on your long ruler, align it with the edge of the fabric and cut off the corner at a 45-degree angle. The fabric should be opened, cutting through a single layer (Figure 1).

2 Set the corner aside for another use, and cut binding strips from the remainder of the fabric (Figure 2a), folding the fabric along the cut edge as needed to shorten the cut (Figure 2b).

3 After the strips have been cut, join the angled ends exactly as shown (Figure 3a). Sew from the "V" at the top of the strip to the "V" at the bottom of the strip (the seam allowance does not have to be ¼"). Join all the strips in this manner to make a continuous binding strip. Press the seams open (Figure 3b).

4 To make a double binding, fold the binding in half, wrong sides together, and press (Figure 4).

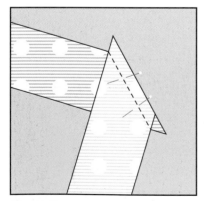

Figure 3a

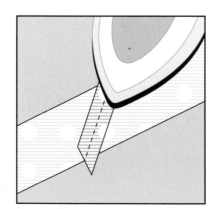

Figure 3b

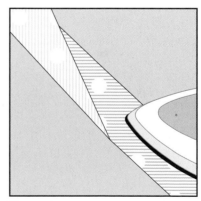

Figure 4

MITERING CORNERS ON BINDING

1 When the quilting is completed, baste a scant ¼" around the perimeter of the quilt to prevent the layers from shifting while the binding is being sewn on. This prevents the edge from stretching. Leave the excess batting and backing in place until after the binding is sewn on, so you can trim off the exact amount needed to completely fill the binding (Figure 1).

2 Begin sewing the binding to the quilt in the middle of one side, matching the raw edges of the binding to the raw edge of the quilt top. Leave a 6" to 8" tail at the beginning (Figure 2).

3 To miter a corner, stitch to within a seam's allowance from the corner, stop and backstitch (Figure 3).

4 Remove the quilt from under the presser foot and trim the threads. Turn the quilt 90-degrees, and pull the binding straight up, forming a 45-degree angle at the corner (Figure 4).

5 Fold the binding back down, with the fold on the previously stitched edge of the quilt. Begin stitching at the fold. This will build in enough extra binding to turn the corner (Figure 5).

6 For corners that are not square (such as on a table runner), stitch the first edge, stop a seam allowance from the corner, and remove the quilt from under the presser foot. Pull the binding straight up, then fold it back down along the next edge. The fold should now come right to the corner of the quilt. It will not align with the previous edge as in a square corner, but rather at right angles to the next edge. Begin stitching at the previous edge.

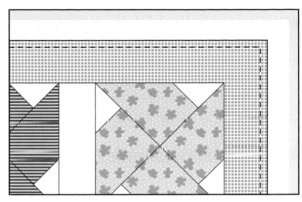

Figure 1

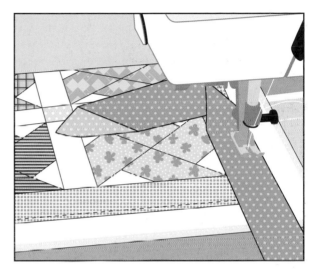

Figure 2

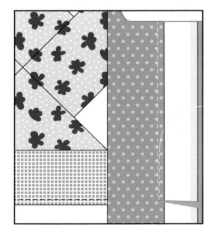

Figure 3

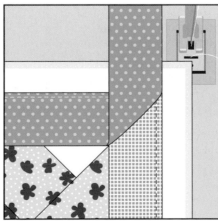

Figure 4

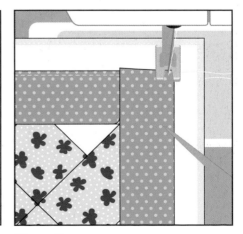

Figure 5

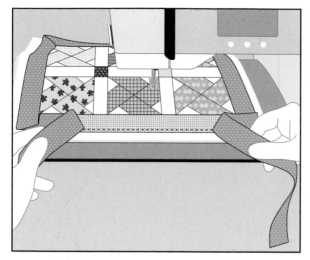

Figure 1

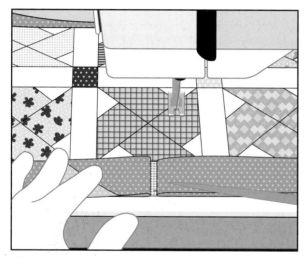

Figure 2

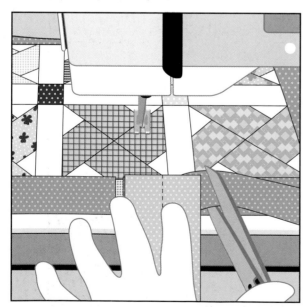

Figure 3

"PERFECT FIT" BINDING

1 When you are within 8" to 10" of where you began binding, stop stitching. Remove the quilt from under the presser foot and trim the threads (Figure 1).

2 On a flat surface, have the binding ends meet in the center of that unstitched area, leaving a scant ¼" between them. Fold the ends over and crease them where they almost meet (Figure 2).

3 Cut one end off at the fold. Then, using the end you have just cut off (open it, if it is a double binding), use it to measure a binding's width away from the fold. Cut off the second end at that measurement (Figure 3).

4 Join the ends at right angles with right sides together. Stitch a diagonal seam. Check if the seam is sewn correctly before trimming it to a ¼" seam allowance. Finger press the seam open, and reposition the binding on the quilt (Figure 4).

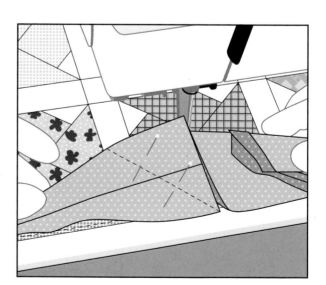

Figure 4

5 Finish stitching the binding to the edge of the quilt (Figure 5).

6 Trim the excess batting and backing. On the top side of the quilt, press the binding away from the edge of the quilt to make it easier to stitch on the back side (Figure 6).

7 On the backside of the quilt, fold the binding over the edge so it covers the stitching line. Hand-sew or machine-sew the binding in place with matching thread (Figure 7).

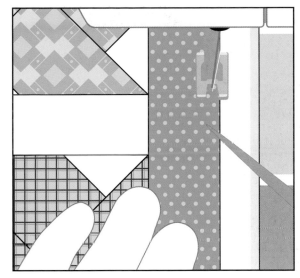

Figure 5

TRY THIS!

- Use appliqué sharps to hand-stitch the binding. These long, thin needles are designed for this type of stitching.
- When stitching the binding down by hand, keep the body of the quilt away from you holding only the binding edge. You'll find it easier to stitch.
- Use binding clips instead of stick pins to hold the binding edge down for sewing. This is simply to avoid poking yourself!

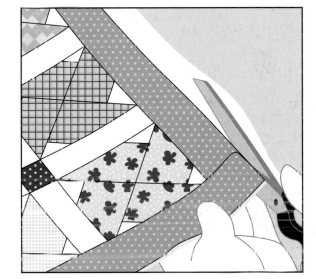

Figure 6

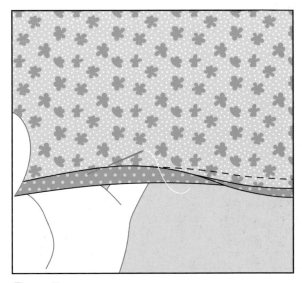

Figure 7

BINDING A SCALLOPED OR CURVED EDGE

Do not cut on the marked line! Quilt, then before binding, hand-baste along the marked line to keep the layers from shifting when the binding is attached. A bias binding is a must for binding curved edges. Cut a 1¼" single bias binding. (Refer to page 10 for detailed instructions on preparing binding.)

1 With raw edges of the binding aligned with the marked line on your quilt, begin sewing a ¼" seam. Stitch to the base of the "V", stop with the needle down and lift the presser foot.

2 Pivot the quilt and binding around the needle. Put the presser foot down and begin stitching out of the "V", taking care not to stitch any pleats into the binding (Figure1).

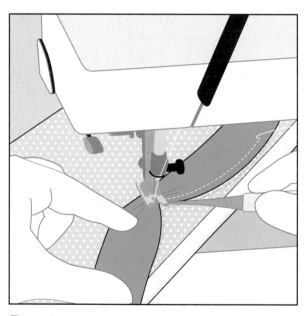

Figure 1

3 Continue around the quilt in this manner, easing the binding around the curves and pivoting at the inside of the "V".

4 Trim the seam allowance an even ¼", turn to the backside and stitch down by hand with matching thread, covering the stitching line. At the "V", the binding will just fold over upon itself, making a little pleat.

QUILT LABELS

Your quilts are your legacy—sign them! A label should include the following:
- Quilt recipient and quilt maker
- Date of completion/presentation
- Where the quilt was made
- Special occasion or story

You can purchase fabric labels or create your own. Sew or appliqué the label to the quilt either before or after the quilt is completed.

FREEZER PAPER APPLIQUÉ

1 Trace the shapes on the dull side of the freezer paper, reversing the image first if necessary. (You can re-use the freezer paper several times.)

2 Cut out the shapes on the marked line. Iron the shapes to the wrong side of the fabrics chosen for the appliqué, leaving at least ¾" between the shapes.

3 Cut out the shapes adding a scant ¼" seam allowance. Clip any inside curves.

4 With equal parts liquid starch and water mixture (or spray starch) and a cotton swab, wet the seam allowance of the appliqué piece. Using the tip of the iron, press the seam allowance over the edge of the freezer paper. Once the edge is well-pressed, remove the freezer paper and iron from the right side.

5 Baste in place on the background square either with needle and thread, or Roxanne's Glue Baste-It.

6 Appliqué down by hand or machine zigzag with matching or invisible thread.

FUSIBLE APPLIQUÉ

1 Trace the reversed pattern on the paper side of fusible web. Leave a bit of space between each appliqué pattern.

2 Cut out, leaving a small excess of paper around the appliqué. For a softer appliqué, cut out the center of the appliqué shape, leaving at least a ¼" margin inside the shape. Iron to the wrong side of the fabrics chosen for the appliqué, following the manufacturer's instructions for fusing.

3 Cut out on the marked line, then peel off the paper backing. Position the appliqué shape in place on the background fabric and fuse in place, following the manufacturer's directions.

4 By machine or hand, buttonhole stitch around the shapes with matching or invisible thread.

EASY ANGLE TOOL

Easy Angle allows you to cut triangles from the same size strip as for squares. You only need to add a ½" seam allowance when using Easy Angle, instead of the 7/8" added when not using the tool.

To use the tool most efficiently, layer the fabric strips you are cutting for your triangles right sides together, then cut with Easy Angle. Now they are ready to be chain-sewn.

Before making the first cut, trim off the selvages. Then align the top flat edge of the tool at the top of the strip, matching a line on the tool with the bottom edge of the strip. Cut on the diagonal edge (Figure 1).

To make the second cut, rotate the tool so the flat edge is aligned at the bottom of the strip, and a line on the tool is aligned with the top of the strip (Figure 2). Cut again.

Continue in this manner down the strip. Chain-sew the triangles on the longest edge. Press toward the darkest fabric and trim the dog-ears.

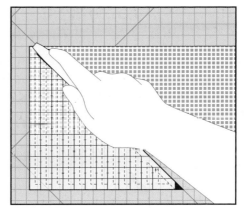

Figure 1

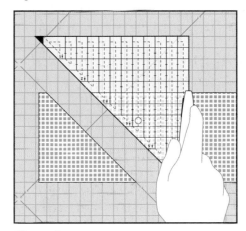

Figure 2

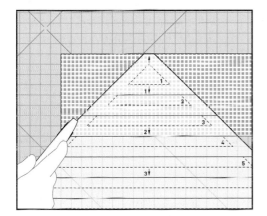

Figure 3

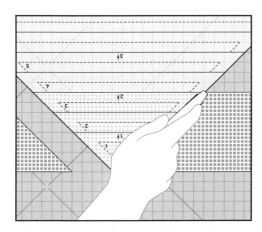

Figure 4

COMPANION ANGLE TOOL

Companion Angle allows you to cut quarter-square triangles with the longest edge on the straight-of-grain. A common use for this type of triangle is the goose in flying geese.

To cut with Companion Angle, align the top flat point of the tool with the top edge of the strip. A line on the tool should align with the bottom of the strip. Cut on both sides of the tool (Figure 3).

For the next cut, rotate the tool so the point of the tool is at the bottom of the strip, and a line on the tool is aligned with the top of the strip. Cut again (Figure 4).

Continue in this manner down the strip of fabric.

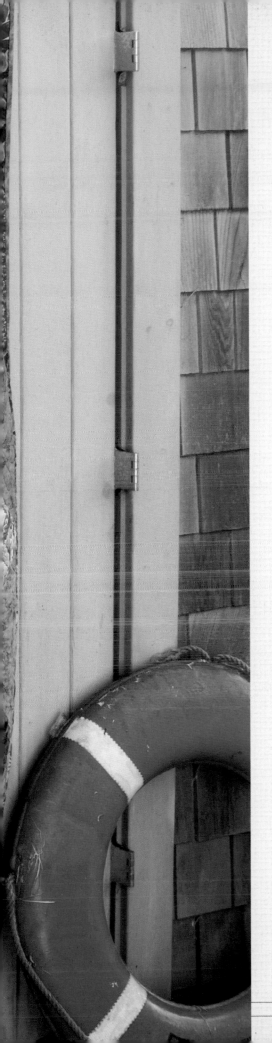

CHAPTER

BREAKING OUT OF THE BOX

Quilting is a creative outlet in every way—pairing fabrics, selecting threads, designing layouts and adding special details like trims and labels. But sometimes even the most creative among us get stuck in a rut or get "quilter's block." You know the symptoms— you can't decide on a pattern, the fabric choices are overwhelming, the perfect print is nowhere to be found and every quilt you make starts to look the same.

The projects in this chapter are the perfect way to help crawl out of your quilting rut. Break out of the box! Try new techniques, use fabrics you've never used before or make a pattern that intimidates you. You'll soon be back to your creative self and able to put your own personal spin on the quilts in this chapter.

From Layer Cake, Jelly Roll and Charm Quilts
by Pam and Nicky Lintott

ELEGANCE

from Black & White and Pieced All Over
by Kay M. Capps Cross

It's sometimes easy to get overwhelmed by the amount and variety of beautiful quilting fabric. This quilt makes choosing fabrics a little easier by utilizing black and white prints and a pop of pink. It is the perfect quilt to hang in a formal sitting or dining room, or to give as a wedding gift. Try making it with a splash of your favorite color!

> ### NEW SKILLS!
>
> Learn how to make continuous bias binding while making this project!

Elegance
Finished quilt: 36" × 47"
Pieced and quilted by
Kay Capps Cross.
Fabrics courtesy of
Maywood Fabrics.

MATERIALS AND CUTTING LIST

MATERIAL	YARDAGE	CUTS	FOR
5 different dark black with white prints	¼ yd. of each (label them a, b, c, d and e)	Cut three 2¼" strips from fabrics a, b, c and d. Cut two 2¼" strips from fabric e.	Fans
Large-scale white with black print	⅞ yd.	Cut two 3" strips. Cut seven 2½" strips; sub-cut into: • seventeen 2½" × 9½" strips	Fan background, Lattice
Medium-scale white with black print	¼ yd.	Cut three 2" strips.	Cornerstone background
Zippy pink	¼ yd.	Cut five 1¼" strips; sub cut into: • two 1¼" × 40½" strips • two 1¼" × 29½" strips • twelve 1¼" × 1¼" strips	Cornerstones, Border
Large-scale very light white with black print	½ yd.	Cut four 3" strips; sub cut into: • two 3" × 40½" strips • two 3" × 24½" strips	Inner border
Large-scale dark black with white print	¾ yd	Cut four 4" strips; sub-cut into: • two 4" × 36½" strips • two 4" × 40½" strips	Outer border
Medium-scale medium black with white print	⅔ yd.	Cut one 20" square.	2¼" continuous bias binding
12"-wide foundation fabric	4½ yds.	Cut six 12" squares. Cut twelve 3" squares.	Foundation piecing
Light large-scale white with black print	1½ yds.	n/a	Backing
Batting	Crib Size	n/a	Batting

ADDITIONAL SUPPLIES

White 8½" × 11" paper (several sheets)

Sulky Iron-On Transfer Pen

Elegance fan and cornerstone patterns on pages 118-120

Figure 1

PREPARATION

1 Enlarge the ELEGANCE patterns (pages 118-120) to the required size. Using an iron-on transfer pen, trace one copy of each section of the fan and cornerstone patterns onto a piece of white paper.

2 Iron the fan patterns directly to each of the six foundation fabric 12" squares.

3 Iron the cornerstone patterns directly to each of the twelve foundation fabric 3" squares.

4 If the ink becomes too faint, retrace the existing lines on the paper with the iron-on pen and keep going!

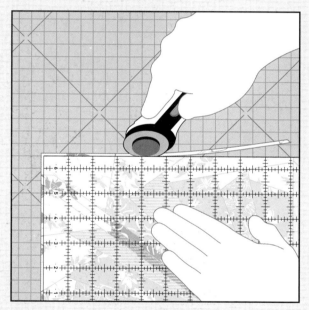

Figure 2

PIECING THE SECTIONS

1 Foundation piece the big fan sections in numerical order using the letters printed on the foundation pattern for fabric placement.

2 Foundation piece the smaller fan sections in numerical order using the letters for fabric placement. Note that e is the only fabric that does not repeat.

3 Press the half blocks, and trim only on the inner cutting lines (Figure 1)

4 Using perpendicular pinning, join the two fan sections and press the seam open.

5 Square the fan blocks to 9½" × 9½" (Figure 2).

6 Foundation piece the cornerstone blocks to make wonky squares in a square (Figure 3). Press the blocks, and square them to 2½" × 2½".

Figure 3

ASSEMBLING THE ROWS

1 Sew a 2½" × 9½" lattice strip to the right-hand side of each fan block (Figure 4). Press the seam allowances toward the lattice.

2 Join two fan blocks with lattice in between to make a row (Figure 5). Repeat to make a total of three rows. Press the seams toward the lattice.

3 Sew a lattice strip to the left side of each row. Press the seam allowances toward the lattice.

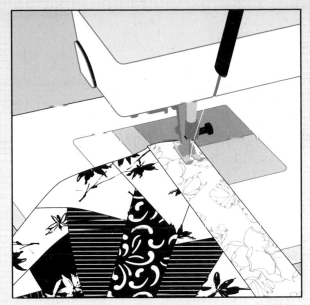

Figure 4

JOINING THE ROWS WITH LATTICE

1 Gather four sets each consisting of three cornerstone blocks (Y) and 2 of the 2" × 8" strips (Z). Sew together one set in this pattern: Y-Z-Y-Z-Y. Repeat for the other three sets (Figure 6).

2 Press the seams toward the lattice.

3 Sew one lattice strip from step 1 to the top of each row of blocks. Press the seams toward the lattice.

4 Sew one lattice strip to the bottom of one row. This is the bottom row. Press the seam toward the lattice.

5 Join the three rows of fans to complete the quilt center. Press the seam allowances toward the lattice.

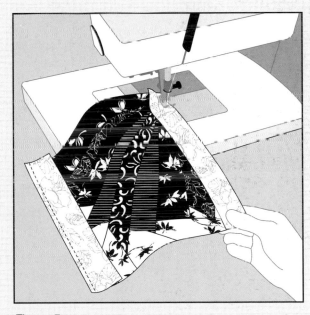

Figure 5

Figure 6

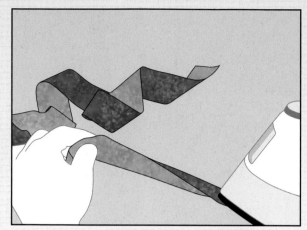

Figure 7

Figure 8

Figure 9

ADDING THE BORDERS

1 Sew one of the 3" × 24½" inner border strips to the top and to the bottom of the quilt center. Press the seams out toward the border.

2 Sew a 3" × 40½" inner border strip to each side of the quilt center. Press the seams out toward the border.

3 Fold and press each zinger border strip in half lengthwise, wrong sides together (Figure 7) .

4 Line up the raw edge of one of the 1¼" × 29½" zinger border strips to the top of the quilt center and then sew to the quilt center with a ⅛" seam. Repeat at the bottom of the quilt center with the other 1¼" × 29½" zinger border strip.

5 Line up the raw edges and sew a 1¼" × 40½" zinger border strip to each side of the quilt center with a ⅛" seam. Do not press these borders out.

6 Sew a 4" × 40½" outer border strip to each side of the quilt center, sandwiching the zinger border (Figure 8).

7 Sew one of the 4" × 36½" outer border strips to the top of the quilt center and one to the bottom, sandwiching the zinger border.

8 Press the seams out toward the border, keeping the zinger borders pointing in toward the quilt center (Figure 9).

MAKING THE CONTINUOUS BIAS BINDING

1 Start with a 20" square of your binding fabric. Make sure the lengthwise grain runs evenly across the top, and the corners are true 90-degrees. Fold the square in half (right-sides together), opposite corners together, creating a triangle. Line up the triangle point and the center of the fold, cut (Figure 10). This produces two triangles.

2 With right sides together, match up the two straight-grain edges to make a pair of triangle pants. Sew that seam from edge to edge (Figure 11). (This produces a parallelogram for all you geometry buffs.) Press the seam open.

3 Lay one of the points flat on a cutting board and make a leader cut the width of your binding and approximately 3 inches long. I use 2¼" binding (Figure 12).

4 Grab the new point created by cutting the leader, and line that straight-grain edge up with the opposite straight-grain edge, right sides together. Let the new point stick past the opposite corner to start the ¼" seam. The leader strip will be hanging loose. Once the seam is sewn, it becomes a tube (Figure 13).

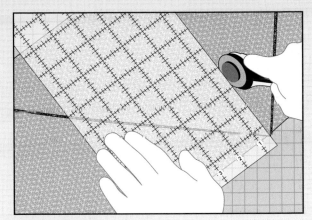

Figure 10

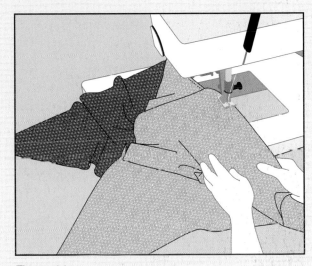

Figure 11

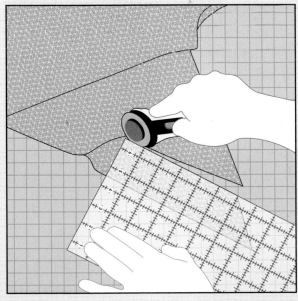

Figure 12

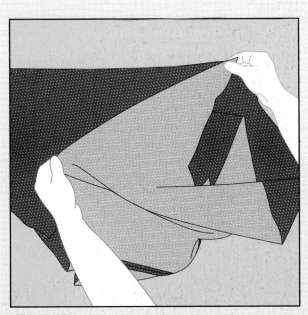

Figure 13

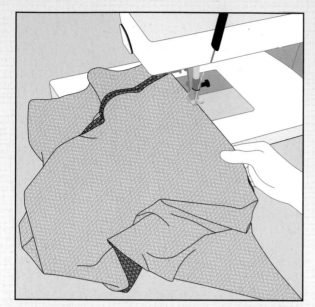

Figure 14

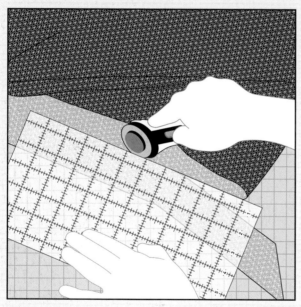

Figure 15

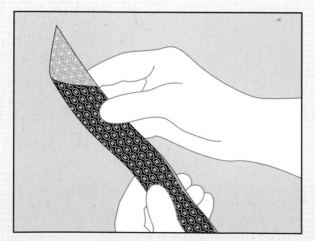

Figure 16

5 Sew the seam together and press open (Figure 14).

6 Starting at the leader strip, cut the continuous strip 2¼" wide (Figure 15). Just keep cutting and cutting, the end is near!

7 With wrong sides together, fold the strip in half lengthwise and press (Figure 16)

TRY THIS!

My grandmother taught me to roll my binding around an empty spool or cardboard cereal box. This keeps it pressed and ready to attach at a moment's notice.

LAYERING, QUILTING AND BINDING

1 Layer, quilt and bind your creation. When using fabrics this busy, the quilting is going to show only as texture, unless you use contrasting thread. I like to stay out of the way of the fabric and let it do the work. I basically quilted the piece to hold it together and add some dimension, not to add design elements.

2 Take pride in your work by signing and dating the quilt or attaching a personalized label to it.

About the Author

Kay M. Capps Cross, popular workshop instructor and designer of Cross Cuts patterns, has written *A Black-and-White Garden* and *Black-and-White Quilts by Design* published by AQS. *Black & White and Pieced All Over* and *Quilted Panels in Black & White* are published by Krause Publications. Kay's quilts are also frequently featured in magazines. She enjoys teaching and sharing her love of black and white along with "stress-free" quilting.

Visit Kay at www.crosscutsquilting.com, www.crosscuts.cc, and crosscuts@springrove.coop.

BAINBRIDGE DELFT

from Bargello Quilts with a Twist
by Maggie Ball

If you've always been too intimidated to try making a bargello quilt, now's the time to be courageous! This quilt features an easy 16-piece bargello block, in which only four strips are sewn at a time. Twist and turn these blocks to create many different layouts, and play with color and value variations in your fabric choices to add another layer of visual appeal.

Bainbridge Delft
Finished quilt: 51" × 51"
Pieced by Maggie Ball.
Machine quilted by
Wanda Rains.

MATERIALS AND CUTTING LIST

NOTE: CUT STRIPS ACROSS THE FULL WIDTH OF THE FABRIC, SELVAGE TO SELVAGE (40"), EXCEPT FOR WHITE/BLUE FLORAL.

MATERIAL	YARDAGE	CUTS	FOR
Dark floral fabric	2 yds.	Cut three 3½" × 40" strips; Label them A1. See "Making the Other Components" for setting triangle and border cutting instructions.	Bargello blocks, Setting triangles, Outer border, Binding
White/blue floral fabric	1⅓ yds.	Cut four 2¼" × 48" lengthwise border strips. Cut three 2½" × 40" lengthwise strips. Label them A2. Cut two 3½" × 40" lengthwise strips. Label them B1.	Bargello blocks, Inner border
Periwinkle dot fabric	⅓ yd.	Cut three 1¾" × 40" strips. Label them A3. Cut one 3½" × 40" strip. Label it C1.	Bargello blocks
Blue floral fabric	½ yd.	Cut two 2½" × 40" strips. Label them B2. Cut one 1¾" × 40" strip. Label it C3. Cut one 1¼" × 40" strip. Label it D4.	Bargello blocks, Middle border
White fabric	½ yd.	Cut three 1¼" × 40" strips. Label them A4. Cut two 1¾" × 40" strips. Label them B3. Cut one 2½" × 40" strip. Label it C2. Cut one 3½" × 40" strip. Label it D1.	Bargello blocks
Dark blue mono fabric	¼ yd.	Cut two 1¼" × 40" strips. Label them B4. Cut one 2½" × 40" strip. Label it D2.	Bargello blocks
Light blue floral fabric	¼ yd.	Cut one 1¼" × 40" strip. Label it C4. Cut one 1¾" × 40" strip. Label it D3.	Bargello blocks
Backing	55" × 55"	n/a	Backing
Batting	55" × 55"	n/a	Batting

A1	B1	C1	D1
A2	B2	C2	D2
A3	B3	C3	D3
A4	B4	C4	D4

Figure 1

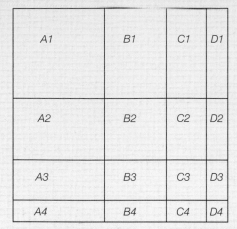

Figure 2 (A Strip Set)

Figure 3

Figure 4

MAKING THE BARGELLO BLOCKS

The bargello block is composed of sixteen patches grouped in four segments: the A, B, C and D segments. Each segment is created by sub-cutting the A, B, C and D strip sets, made by strip piecing four full-width strips of fabric. See Figure 1 for layout.

1 Strip piece an A strip set. Right sides together, sew an A1 strip to an A2 strip lengthwise. In the same manner, sew an A3 strip to an A4 strip. Press the seams open and stitch the pairs of strips together, again pressing the seam open to complete an A set. Repeat to make two more A strip sets.

2 Following the instructions in step 1, piece two B strip sets, one C strip set, and one D strip set, making sure that the strips are joined in numerical order. Press seams open.

3 You should have three A strip sets, two B strip sets and one each of C and D before you make the sub-cuts. Sub-cut the A sets 3½" (Figure 2), the B sets 2½", the C set 1¾" and the D set 1¼": twenty-four segments of each (Figure 3). The C set will yield only twenty-two segments.

4 Make two more C segments. From the leftover D strip set, make two sub-cuts 1¾". Rip apart the pieces at the joining seams, and trim the pieces to the correct size: D1 becomes C2 (1¾" x 2½"), D2 becomes C3 (1¾" x 1¾"), D3 becomes C4 (1¾" x 1¼"). Cut two C1 sections separately (1¼" x 3½"). Sew the pieces into two C segments.

5 Join one A segment to a B segment. Then sew a C segment to a D segment. Press the seams open and join the pairs of segments, once again pressing the final seam open to complete the 7" bargello block (Figure 4). Always place the smaller of the two segments on the top and stitch from the widest (#1 piece) to the narrowest (#4 piece). Repeat to make twenty-four identical bargello blocks.

MAKING THE OTHER COMPONENTS

1 Cut the four outer border strips (54" × 3") lengthwise from the dark floral fabric.

2 From the same fabric, cut four 12" squares for the setting and corner triangles. Cut two of the dark floral 12" squares into quarters by cutting diagonally both ways. This makes eight setting triangles. Cut the other two dark floral 12" squares in half diagonally to make four corner triangles.

3 Lay out the blocks in the desired configuration with the setting and corner triangles; use Figure 5 as a guide or create your own pattern.

Figure 5

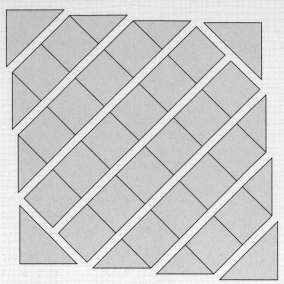

Figure 6

ASSEMBLING THE QUILT

1 Assemble the center field of the quilt, joining the components in diagonal rows (Figure 6). Trim away the excess from the sides, leaving ¼" seam allowances all the way around (Figure 7).

2 You should already have the inner and outer border strips cut. Cut and join five full-width 1¼" strips for the middle blue floral borders to make four (50" × 1¼") strips. Strip piece the inner, middle and outer border strips; join them to the quilt top, mitering the corners if you would like (see page 116 for more instruction on mitering borders). Alternatively, add each border in turn, measuring across the center of the quilt to accurately determine strip lengths. Join the sides first and then the tops and bottoms.

3 Baste, quilt and bind (see pages 9–13). Binding strips (2½" recommended) may may be cut lengthwise from the remaining dark floral fabric. BAINBRIDGE DELFT has an overall floral quilting pattern.

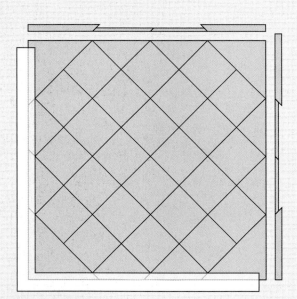

Figure 7

TRY THIS!

Try making this block in different fabric combinations, and play with the arrangement and orientation of the blocks. The possibilities are endless!

About the Author

Maggie Ball began quilting in 1986 and enjoys creating her own designs from elements of traditional patterns. Her award-winning quilts have been exhibited nationally and overseas. Teaching quilting is a natural extension of her passion and she finds it rewarding. Her teaching experience is extensive in the USA, and beyond to the UK and Mongolia, as well as quilting with over 800 children in local schools. Maggie's books *Creative Quilting with Kids* and *Patchwork and Quilting with Kids* aim to encourage adults to pass on the quilting tradition to the next generation. *Traditional Quilts with a Twist* contains new patterns derived from traditional blocks. Her most recent book, *Bargello Quilts with a Twist*, features quilts made from her original, easy to construct, 16-piece bargello block.

For more information on the Mongolian project and the classes and lectures Maggie offers, visit her website at www.dragonflyquilts.com.

SPINNING WHEEL

from Simple Stained Glass Quilts
by Susan Purney Mark and Daphne Greig

Impress all of your quilting friends with this stained glass quilt. Break away from traditionally pieced patchwork and try something out of the ordinary. This beautiful small quilt utilizes a super-simple appliqué technique that makes this intricate quilt fast and easy to complete.

NEW SKILLS!

Learn a new fusible web technique for leading while you make this quilt!

Spinning Wheel
Finished quilt: 28¾" × 28¾"
Pieced and quilted by Daphne Greig.

MATERIALS AND CUTTING LIST

MATERIAL	YARDAGE	CUTS	FOR
2 complementary focus fabrics	½ yd. each	From both fabrics, cut: • Two 6½" squares • Two 5½" squares • Four 6½" × 5½" rectangles	Block background
Contrasting fabric	2½ yds.	Cut one 30" square.	Leading, Backing, Binding
Batting (low-loft)	32" × 32"	n/a	Batting

ADDITIONAL SUPPLIES

Fusible web (four 12" squares)

60 Weight machine embroidery thread (to match leading fabric)

White ink marker

SPINNING WHEEL pattern on page 121

Sheet of parchment paper (to protect ironing board surface)

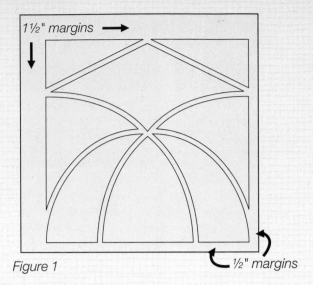

1½" margins →

↓

½" margins

Figure 1

Figure 2

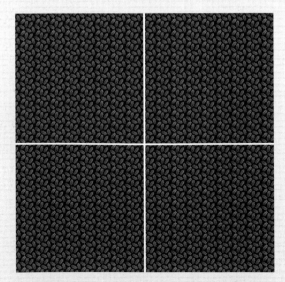

Figure 3

PREPARING THE LEADING

1 Enlarge and trace the SPINNING WHEEL pattern from page 121 onto the paper side of a fusible web square, leaving ½" on the right and bottom edges and 1½" at the top and left edges (Figure 1). Repeat for the remaining three squares. Smoothly trace the curves and use a ruler to trace the straight lines.

2 Trim the right and bottom edge of each square to ⅛" from the edge of the design (Figure 2).

3 Press the 30" square of leading fabric well to remove puckers and wrinkles.

4 Draw centered vertical and horizontal placement lines on the wrong side of the leading fabric square with a white ink marker (Figure 3). These lines will be used to align the traced fusible squares.

NOTE: DO NOT PRESS THE FABRIC AFTER DRAWING THE PLACEMENT LINES BECAUSE THE WHITE INK MARKER WILL BE REMOVED WITH THE HEAT AND STEAM FROM YOUR IRON.

5 Place one square of fusible web on the wrong side of the leading fabric in the top left area. Line up the trimmed edges of the fusible web with the drawn lines (Figure 4).

6 Cover the fusible web with your pressing sheet and fuse, following the web manufacturer's instructions. Be sure all edges are fused well.

7 Place a second square of fusible web right next to the first one, turning the square a quarter turn (Figure 5). The two squares meet will be exactly ¼" apart (⅛" on each square of fusible web).

8 Cover the fusible web with your pressing sheet and fuse. Be sure all edges are fused well.

9 Place and fuse the third and fourth squares of fusible web in the remaining areas, one at a time, turning the squares to continue the established pattern (Figure 6).

10 Let the piece cool. Use your rotary cutter, scissors or art knife to cut the open areas of the design. Be sure to cut smooth curves and maintain the ¼" leading lines, and use a ruler when cutting the straight lines.

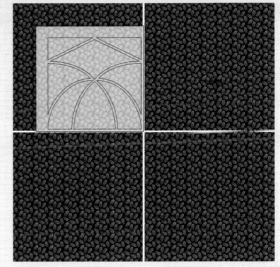

Figure 4

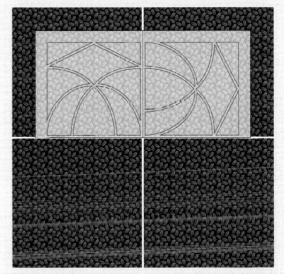

Figure 5

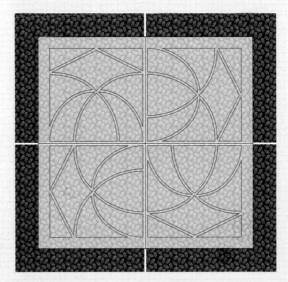

Figure 6

MAKING THE QUILT TOP

1 With your focus fabric squares and rectangles, arrange the quilt top (Figure 7) alternating the two fabrics. Sew pieces together with ¼" seam allowances. Press all allowances open.

2 Place a piece of parchment paper on your ironing surface so your quilt will not be fused to the surface (there will be excess fusible around the edges of the focus fabric).

3 Place the focus fabric piece right side up on your pressing surface. Carefully remove the paper backing and position the leading over the focus fabric. Place the center vertical and horizontal leading lines on top of the center seams of the pieced fabric.

4 Cover the leading with your pressing sheet and fuse it to the focus fabric. Be careful that you don't move the leading during this step. Let the fused fabrics cool.

5 With the piece right side up, measure 4½" away from the outer edges of the fabric and trim the excess leading fabric.

QUILTING AND FINISHING

1 Cut a 32" × 32" piece of leading fabric for the backing.

2 Sandwich the quilt top, batting and backing together and baste well with safety pins.

3 Thread your sewing machine in the top and bobbin with embroidery thread to match the leading fabric. Set your machine to a narrow zigzag stitch.

4 Begin in the center of the quilt and stitch on both edges of each leading line. Remove pins as necessary while you sew.

5 Remove all remaining pins and square up the wall hanging.

6 Cut four strips of leading fabric 2¼" wide for binding. Join the strips on the short ends with 45-degree seams. Press the seam allowances open to reduce bulk.

7 Fold the binding in half lengthwise, wrong sides together, and apply the binding all around the raw edges, mitering the corners.

8 Turn the binding to the back and slipstitch in place by hand.

9 Add a sleeve and label to the back of your wall hanging.

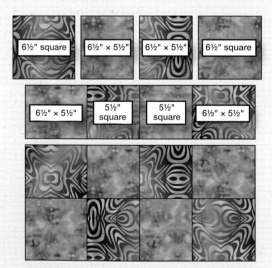

Figure 7

TRY THIS!

Try using variegated polyester thread (coordinated with the focus fabrics) and a wave stitch to quilt the wide outer border.

About the Authors

Susan and Daphne began working together when they met over the cutting table of their local quilt shop more than twelve years ago. They formed their company, Patchworks Studio, and began designing and publishing patterns together shortly afterward. They have been creating their Too Easy Stained Glass patterns since 2003. They teach the technique all across North America to excited quiltmakers who loudly exclaim, "It's too easy!" They love bringing a variety of designs and techniques into print in books, patterns and magazines and have a great many ideas stored up for future publication.

Susan and Daphne live in Victoria, British Columbia, where they love to garden, walk and explore their beautiful native land. They also spend part of each year traveling and teaching. Visit them at www.patchworkstudio.com.

LA BOHEMIA WALL QUILT

from Log Cabin Quilts with Attitude
by Sharon V. Rotz

The traditional log cabin block gets a modern makeover in this bright and folksy quilt. If you love the log cabin but are ready to break out of the box, here's your chance. Even better, you'll get to use up those scraps you can't part with! This wall hanging has a little something for every quilter—a hint of traditional, a modern twist, appliqué, piecing and the opportunity to embellish with your favorite trim.

NEW SKILLS!

Learn to make a free-style log cabin block while making this quilt.

La Bohemia Wall Quilt

Finished quilt: 51" × 51"
*Pieced and quilted by
Sharon V. Rotz.*

MATERIALS AND CUTTING LIST

NOTE: BEFORE CUTTING, READ THE COMPLETE INSTRUCTIONS.
FOR ALL APPLIQUÉ SHAPES, READ STEPS 1 THROUGH 6 FIRST.

MATERIAL	YARDAGE	CUTS	FOR
Assorted brightly colored prints and solids	2 yds.	As needed, cut 1" to 2½" wide strips	Freedom blocks
Medium to dark yellow fabric	1½ yds.	Cut two 4" x 51½" strips (lengthwise). Cut two 4" x 44½" strips (lengthwise). Cut three strips, 1½" x width or length; sub-cut into: • twelve 1½" x 6½" rectangles	Borders, Border 3 spacers
Medium yellow fabric	1 yd.	Cut two 5½" x WOF strips; sub-cut into: • four 5½" x 20½" strips Cut one 5½" x WOF strip; sub-cut into: • four 5½" squares Cut three 1½" x WOF strips; sub-cut into: • twelve 1½" x 6½" rectangles	Border 2, Border 3 spacers
Red/print 1	1 yd.	Cut six 3½" x WOF strips; sub-cut into: • sixty 3½" squares Cut four small flowers. From remainder, cut 1" to 2½" wide strips.	Prairie points, Border 2 appliqué, Freedom blocks
Blue/print 1	¾ yd.	Cut six 2¼" x WOF strips; piece to needed binding length. Cut two birds (one regular, one reversed). From remainder, cut strips 1" to 2½" wide.	Binding, Center appliqué, Freedom blocks
Red/print 2	½ yd.	Cut two large-sectioned flowers. Cut five small flowers. From remainder, cut 1" to 2½" wide strips.	Center and Border 2 appliqué, Freedom blocks
Multicolored print	¼ yd.	Cut four 2" x 17½" rectangles. From remainder, cut 1" to 2½" wide strips.	Border 1, Freedom blocks
Pale yellow	1 fat quarter	Cut one 17½" square.	Center background
Solid red	1 fat quarter	Cut four large-sectioned flowers. Cut three small flowers. From remainder, cut 1" to 2½" wide strips.	Border 2 appliqué, Freedom blocks
Blue/print 2	1 fat quarter	Cut two single leaves (one regular, one reversed). Cut four double leaves (two regular, two reversed). From remainder, cut 1" to 2½" wide strips.	Center appliqué, Freedom blocks
Blue/print 3	1 fat eighth	Cut four 2" squares. From remainder, cut 1" to 2½" wide strips.	Border 1 corners, Freedom blocks
Backing fabric	3 yds., or forty-nine 8½" squares	n/a	Backing
Batting	54" x 54"	n/a	Batting

ADDITIONAL SUPPLIES

7 yds. red medium rickrack (binding, flowers)
4½ yds. blue medium rickrack (border 2, birds)
3 yds. paper-backed fusible adhesive web
Invisible thread (for attaching rickrack)

Decorative thread (appliqué)
6½" or larger ruler
Clear-drying fabric glue
LA BOHEMIA WALL QUILT patterns on pages 122-123

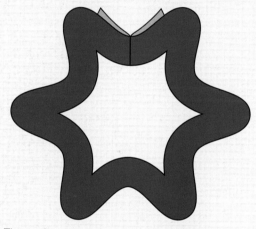

Figure 1

Figure 2

Figure 3

CONSTRUCTING THE CENTER APPLIQUÉ

1 Lightly press the pale yellow background into quarters (Figure 1). This will help you to place the appliqué shapes.

2 Trace one bird and one reversed bird on the paper side of the fusible web. Rough cut around the shapes, and fuse them to the wrong side of the blue/ print 1 fabric. Trim the shapes, and remove the paper. Position the shapes on the appliqué background.

3 Trace all of the single and double leaves on the paper side of the fusible web. Fuse the shapes to the blue/print 2 fabric.

4 Trace one small flower, one sectioned flower and one reversed sectioned flower on the fusible web. Fuse the traced shapes to the red/print 2 fabric. Trim the shapes, and place the leaves and flowers on the background.

5 Trace the flower center circle on fusible web, and fuse it to a small-scale dark print. Trim the shape, and place it in the center of the flower.

6 Fuse all of the shapes onto the background and appliqué in place. A blanket stitch (1.5 length x 2.0 width) and rayon decorative thread were used on the quilt shown. Make adjustments to your machine as needed to accommodate different needle types, threads and stitch lengths. Secure the threads by pulling the ends to the wrong side and tying them.

7 Cut a 6" piece of red rickrack to make a circle with six points. Fold the rickrack in half and stitch a seam, keeping the edges even (Figure 2). Backstitch at both ends to secure the stitching. Press the seam open. Press the rickrack into a flat circle, and hide the ends of the rickrack by trimming the seam allowance and gluing the ends out of sight (Figure 3). Make two. Use invisible thread to stitch the circles to the centers of the sectioned flowers.

8 Cut a 6" piece of blue rickrack. Press it into a curved shape to create a wing. Apply clear-drying glue to the ends of the rickrack to keep it from raveling. Make two. Place the rickrack wings on the birds; use invisible thread to stitch them in place (Figure 4).

Figure 4

CONSTRUCTING BORDER 2 APPLIQUÉ

1 Trace four sectioned flowers on the paper side of the fusible web (Figure 5). Fuse the web to the wrong side of the solid red fabric. Trim the shapes, remove the paper and center the flowers on the two 5½" yellow border corner squares. Fuse in place, and appliqué.

2 Trace four flower center circles on the paper side of the fusible web. Fuse the web to the wrong side of a small-scale dark print. Trim the shapes, remove the paper and fuse a circle in each flower center. Appliqué the circles in place.

3 Cut 6" pieces of red rickrack. Make rickrack circles as you did for the center appliqué. Stitch the circles in place on the corner sectioned flowers.

4 For the side borders, trace twelve small flowers on the fusible web. Fuse four flowers on the wrong side of red/print 1, five flowers on the wrong side of red/print 2 and three flowers on the wrong side of the red solid.

5 Trim the small flowers. Randomly mix the flowers, and fuse three on each side border. Lightly press the border in half to determine the center; place one flower on the center line. Place the other two flowers 6" from the center (Figure 6).

6 Appliqué the small flowers in place. If desired, cut and fuse center circles for the flowers.

MAKING THE FREEDOM BLOCKS

To make a freedom block, you'll need a square or rectangular center and strips to wrap around it. Try piecing your centers for an added touch. Use the fabrics indicated in the cutting chart.

1 Place the first strip right side up under the machine. Place a center piece wrong side up on the strip, and stitch a seam (Figure 7).

2 Press the seam allowance away from the center. Trim away the excess strip so it is even with the edge of the center.

3 Place the second strip under the machine, right side up. Place the block right sides together on the strip with the first strip that you attached at the top. Stitch. Press away from the center and trim even with the edge of the block (Figure 8).

Figure 5

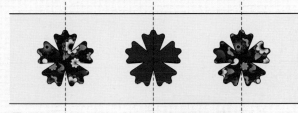

Figure 6

Figure 7

Figure 8

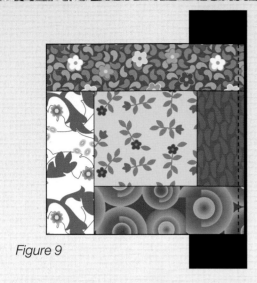

Figure 9

4 Repeat to add strips to the third and fourth side of your block.

5 After making the first complete circle of the log cabin block, check your work. Place the block on strip #5. Look at the wrong side of the block; there will be no seam on the top edge and two seams on the stitching edge (Figure 9).

6 Continue to add random strips around the block; the block will begin to show its personality. The center of the block may no longer be in the middle because the strips on one side may be wider than the other.

7 Use a rotary cutter and ruler to shape up wavy edges on the block. If you feel that a strip is too wide after you have stitched it on, trim that strip down to size.

8 Add strips until the block is approximately 8". Make twenty-four freedom blocks.

FINISHING THE FREEDOM BLOCKS

Trim all of your blocks to 6½" squares, skewing twelve blocks left and twelve blocks right.

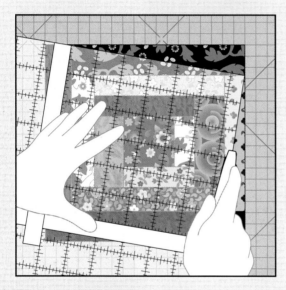

Figure 10

1 Use tape to mark the 6½" cutting lines on your square ruler.

2 Lay the ruler on the block so that the ruler is tilted higher on the left side than it is on the right. Tilt the ruler to a random angle that fits the size of the block (Figure 10). If you can't tilt the block at least ½", add a few more strips to it. Too small of a cut angle will make the block look like a crooked square, while too large of an angle will put the block on point.

3 Make sure that you are cutting on the correct lines, that you have fabric under all of the corners of the taped lines, and that you have laid the square ruler at an interesting angle. Cut the two outer sides of the block.

4 Rotate the block 180-degrees, and line it up with the taped lines. Cut the other two sides of the block. Cut twelve freedom blocks skewed to the left in this way.

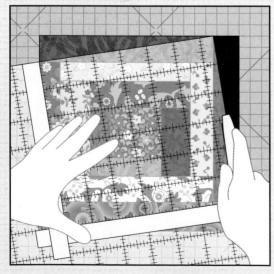

Figure 11

5 Follow the above steps, except this time tilt the ruler so that it is higher on the right side (Figure 11). Trim twelve freedom blocks skewed to the right.

ADDING THE BORDERS

1 Sew on the inner side borders. Then add a blue corner to each end of the top and bottom borders. Stitch the top and bottom borders to the center (Figure 12). Press.

2 Sew on the outer side borders. Add a flowered corner to each end of the top and bottom borders. Stitch the top and bottom borders to the quilt top (Figure 13). Press.

3 Starting with a left block in the corner, alternate laying out left- and right-skewed freedom blocks around the quilt top.

4 Stitch a yellow 1½" x 6½" spacer to the inside edge of each right freedom block as shown (Figure 14).

5 Stitch a medium/dark yellow 1½" x 6½" spacer to the outside edge of each left freedom block. Stitch a 1½" x 7½" spacer to the second outside edge of the four corner freedom blocks (Figure 15).

6 Stitch the side blocks together, and add them to the sides of the quilt top. Stitch the top and bottom blocks together, and add them to the top and bottom of the quilt.

7 Cut a 146" length of rickrack. Piece the ends together to make a circle. Make sure the rickrack is twist-free before you seam the ends. Pin the rickrack loop in place, weaving in and out between the flowers. Use invisible thread to stitch the rickrack onto the quilt top (Figure 16).

8 Stitch the 4" x 44½" medium/dark yellow borders to the sides of the quilt top. Stitch the 4" x 51½" medium/dark yellow borders to the top and bottom of the quilt top.

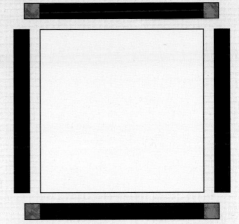

Figure 12

Figure 13

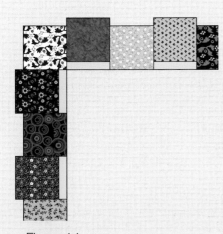

Figure 14

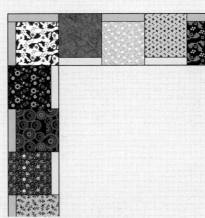

Figure 15

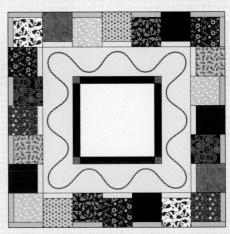

Figure 16

fold

1¾"

3½"

Figure 17

Figure 18

Figure 19

Figure 20

FINISHING

1 Piece the backing. Trim the finished backing to 54" x 54".
Optional Backing: For added interest, piece the backing using 8½" squares (cut size) of gaily printed fabrics. You will need forty-nine total squares.

2 Layer the backing, batting and quilt top. Baste the layers for quilting.

3 Quilt as desired, or try these suggestions.

Center: Echo quilt each shape, and cross-hatch the background.
Border 1: Quilt ¼" from the rickrack, and stitch in the ditch between borders 1 and 2.
Border 2: Echo quilt the appliqué and rickrack.
Border 3: Try a skewed cross-hatch pattern.
Border 4: Quilt a flower vine, using the appliqué flower shapes as patterns.

4 Add the prairie points. Fold the 3½" squares of red/print 2 in half, wrong sides together (Figure 17). Keep the folded edge on top, and fold the right corner to the center (Figure 18). Repeat with the left corner. All of the raw edges should now be on the bottom. Press. Baste the bottom edges of the prairie points (Figure 19).

5 Pin the prairie points on the right side of the quilt top, pointing to the center of the quilt. Pin fifteen on each side.

6 Add rickrack over the prairie points. Center it ¼" from the edge so that half of the rickrack will show when you stitch on your binding (Figure 20).

7 Use the 2¼" strips for the binding; this binding was cut a little wider to accommodate the extra thickness of the prairie points and rickrack.

About the Author

Sharon V. Rotz shares her love of fabric and passion for color through teaching and encouraging the appreciation of quilting as an art form. She has written three Krause Publications books: *Log Cabin Quilts with Attitude, Quilting through the Seasons* and *Serge and Merge Quilts*. A home economics education graduate, Sharon's quilting reflects varied skills learned in the ready-made clothing, tailoring and home decor fields.

Visit Sharon online at www.bysher.net.

TWISTING THE NIGHT AWAY

from Layer Cake, Jelly Roll and Charm Quilts
by Pam and Nicky Lintott

If you have always been drawn to the bright, bold and colorful prints of certain designers but just can't figure out how to use them, then this is the quilt for you. This sensational quilt really makes a statement—and it's so easy to make! If you don't already have a collection of larger-than-life prints, you can make this quilt with pre-cut squares.

> ## NEW SKILLS!
>
> Learn to make a twist block without inset seams.

Twisting the Night Away
Finished quilt: 62" × 74"
Pieced by Pam and Nicky Lintott.
Longarm quilted by The Quilt Room.

MATERIALS AND CUTTING LIST

MATERIAL	YARDAGE	CUTS	FOR
Variety of large focal prints	1 layer cake or forty 10" squares	Leave twenty layers uncut; set aside. Choose twelve layers; Cut one 6" strip from each. • Sub-cut each strip into twelve 6" squares. • Save the excess 4" × 10" and 4" × 6" rectangles for the border. From each of the remaining eight layers, cut two 4" × 10" rectangles.	Snowball block centers, Twist block centers, Border
Dark twist fabric	⅔ yd.	Cut eight 2½" strips across the width of fabric. • Sub-cut six strips into twenty-four 2½" x 8" rectangles. • Sub-cut remaining two strips into thirty-one 2½" squares.	Twist blocks
Light twist fabric	2 yds.	Cut eight 2½" strips across the width of fabric. • Sub-cut six strips into twenty-four 2½" x 8" rectangles. • Sub-cut remaining two strips into thirty-one 2½" squares. Cut two 14¾" wide strips across the width of the fabric; sub-cut into four 14¾" squares. • Sub-cut each square twice on the diagonal into 16 setting triangles. Cut one 8" strip; sub-cut into two 8" squares. • Sub-cut both squares on one diagonal into four corner triangles.	Twist blocks, Setting triangles, Corner triangles
Binding fabric	⅔ yd.	Cut eight 2½" strips.	Binding
Backing fabric	66" × 78"	n/a	Backing
Batting	Twin size	n/a	Batting

TRY THIS!

If you're feeling adventurous, try using a contrasting fabric for your corner and setting triangles, rather than using the light twist fabric.

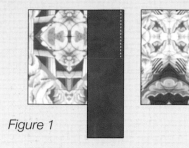

Figure 1

MAKING THE TWIST BLOCKS

1 Take one dark twist rectangle and, with right sides together, sew it only halfway down one side of a 6" square. Press open (Figure 1).

2 With right sides together, sew a light rectangle to the top of the square and press open (Figure 2).

3 With right sides together, sew a dark rectangle to the left side of the square and press open (Figure 3).

4 With right sides together, sew a light rectangle to the bottom of the square and press open (Figure 4).

5 Now sew the first incomplete seam to complete the block. Repeat this process to make twelve twist blocks (Figure 5).

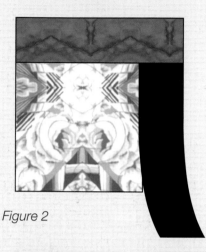

Figure 2

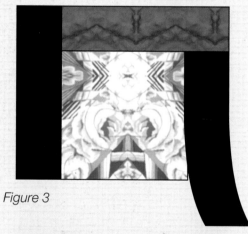

Figure 3

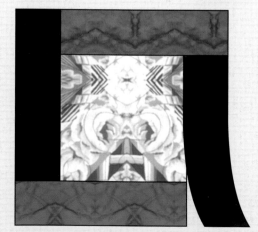

Figure 4

Figure 5

MAKING THE SNOWBALL BLOCKS

1 Draw a diagonal line from corner to corner on the wrong side of a dark 2½" square snowball corner (Figure 6).

2 With right sides together, lay the marked dark square on one corner of a 10" square, aligning the outer edges. Sew across the diagonal, using the marked diagonal line as the stitching line (Figure 7). After awhile, you may find you do not need to draw the line, as it is not difficult to judge the sewing line. Alternatively, make a crease to follow.

3 Open the square out and press toward the outside of the block aligning the raw edges (Figure 8). Fold the corner back down and trim the excess snowball corner fabric but do not trim the layer square. Although this creates a little more bulk, keeping the layer square uncut will keep your unit in shape. Repeat on the other corner (Figure 9).

4 The snowball blocks have two, three or four snowball corners in both light and dark to create the pattern. Refer to Figure 10 for the number of each variation to make.

Figure 6   *Figure 7*

Figure 8   *Figure 9*

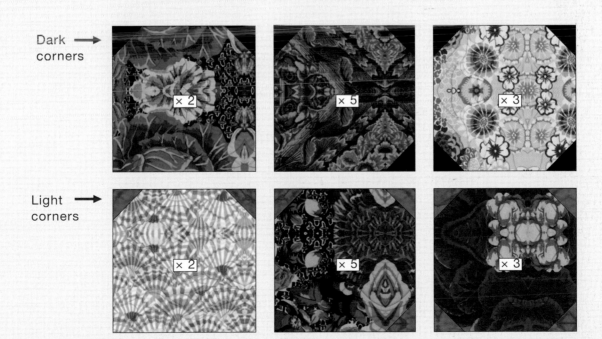

Dark corners →

Light corners →

Figure 10

49

SETTING THE BLOCKS ON POINT

1 Referring to Figure 11, sew a setting triangle to each side of a snowball block with two light corners to create Row 1.

2 Create Row 2 by sewing a snowball block with three dark corners to either side of a twist block with a setting triangle at each end.

3 Continue to sew the blocks together as shown to form rows with a setting triangle at each end. Sew the corner triangles on last.

4 Press toward the snowball block and your seams will nest together nicely.

ADDING THE BORDERS

1 Join together the rectangles you set aside for the border to form a long length. You need a length of about 280", so you will have a few spare.

2 Determine the vertical measurement from top to bottom through the center of your quilt top. Cut two side border strips to this measurement. Placing right sides together, stitch quilt and side borders together, easing the quilt side to fit where necessary.

3 Determine the horizontal measurement from side to side across the center of the quilt top. Cut two top and bottom border strips to this measurement and add to the quilt top in the same manner as before.

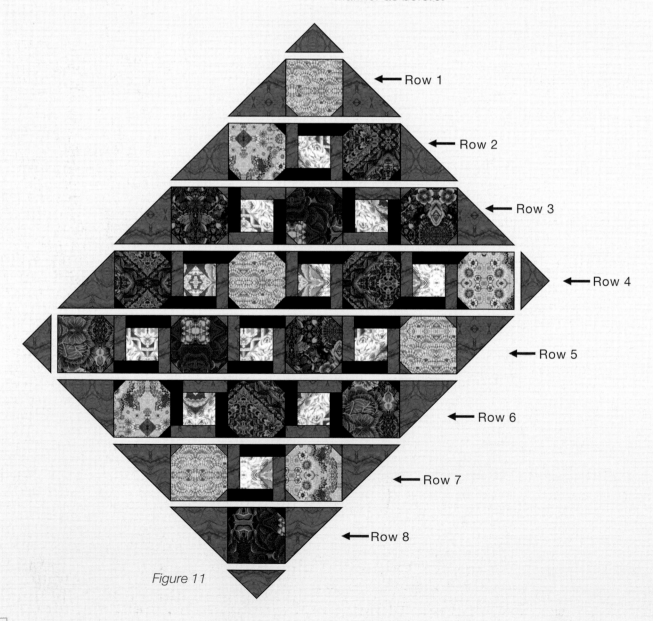

← Row 1

← Row 2

← Row 3

← Row 4

← Row 5

← Row 6

← Row 7

← Row 8

Figure 11

About the Authors

Pam Lintott started The Quilt Room in Dorking, England back in 1981, which she now runs with her daughter, Nicky. Big celebrations are planned as their 30th anniversary approaches! Pam and Nicky have now written four books, including their best-seller *Jelly Roll Quilts*. Their other titles include *Layer Cake, Jelly Roll and Charm Quilts, Jelly Roll Challenge* and *Two From One Jelly Roll Quilts*.

Visit Pam and Nicky at www.quiltroom.co.uk and at their blog (which includes the latest patchwork and quilting information) at www.quiltroom.typepad.co.uk.

FEELING SCRAPPY

If you, like most quilters, have a box in your sewing room full of the bits and pieces of fabric you just can't throw away, then the next five projects are for you. These scrappy quilts oftentimes become our favorites because they are made up of our previous sewing endeavors.

If you hate working with little bits and pieces of fabric, never fear! Make these projects with yardage or pre-cuts that have been lying around your sewing room waiting for the perfect project. A quilt doesn't have to be made out of scraps to still have that scrappy-look.

As you delve into these projects, enjoy the process of combining odds and ends without planning too thoroughly. You'll be amazed with the spontaneous results!

From **Scrap Quilt Sensation**
by Katharine Guerrier

STRIPPIN' IN THE GARDEN

from Sugar Sack Quilts
by Glenna Hailey

This playful scrap quilt is perfect for livening up the walls of a play room, draping over the end of a guest bed or using for a picnic or tea party. The bright rickrack adds a colorful pop, and the variety of fabrics and colors will help brighten up anyone's day. The best part of all—no curved seams or mitered borders!

NEW SKILLS!

Learn a fusible web outline technique while making this project.

Strippin' in the Garden
Finished quilt: 40" × 40"
Pieced by Glenna Hailey.
Longarm quilted by Mary Covey.

MATERIALS AND CUTTING LIST

MATERIAL	YARDAGE	CUTS	FOR
Feedsack scraps	Approx. 2 yds.	Cut lots of random strips 1½"–3" × 6", Cut five 5½" squares. Cut four 2½" x 3½" rectangles.	Pieced blocks, Pieced outer border, Daisies, Small half blossoms
Solid red fabric	½ yd.	Cut eight 7½" squares.	Pieced blocks
Solid white fabric	¾ yd.	Cut four 2" wide strips (selvage to selvage). Cut eight 7½" squares.	Pieced blocks, Inner border
Scraps of coordinating solids	scraps	Cut five 5½" squares. Cut four 3" x 5½" rectangles.	Large blossoms, Large half blossoms
Yellow scraps	scraps	Cut nine 2" squares.	Flower centers
Solid green scraps	⅛ yd.	Cut twenty-eight 2½" x 4" rectangles	Leaves
Backing fabric	2⅝ yds.	n/a	Backing
Red solid fabric	½ yd.	n/a	Binding
Batting	44" × 44"	n/a	Batting

ADDITIONAL SUPPLIES

Large red rickrack (4 yds.)

Lightweight fusible web

Medium-size rickrack in 16 coordinating colors (½ yd. of each color)

STRIPPIN' IN THE GARDEN patterns on page 124

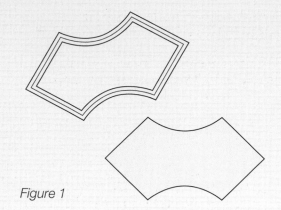

Figure 1

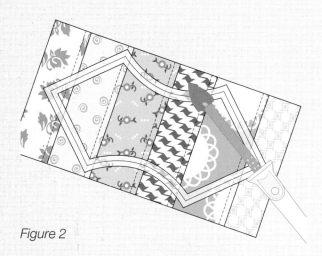

Figure 2

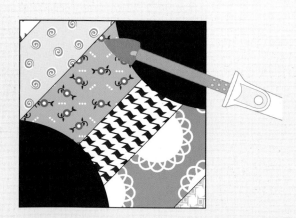

Figure 3

MAKING THE BLOCKS

1 The appliqué patterns for STRIPPIN' IN THE GARDEN are on page 124. Enlarge the patterns to the required size. On the paper side of the fusible web, trace sixteen of the block pattern.

2 Cut the shape out, leaving a small margin (about ⅛") outside the drawn line. Then cut out the center of the shapes to about ⅛" inside the drawn line, leaving an outline in the shape of the pattern piece (Figure 1). This will leave you with enough fusible web to adhere the piece of the background fabric, but it will not leave it stiff to the touch.

3 Using feedsack scraps, sew enough strips together to make a unit at least 6" × 11". Press this strip unit well, seams pressed in the same direction.

4 Press a block pattern web outline on the back of each strip unit (Figure 2).

5 Cut the pieces on the drawn line and remove the paper backing. Handle the pieces carefully to avoid distorting them.

6 Place each strip unit on a 7½" square, lining up the corners. Fuse them in place according to the web manufacturer's directions (Figure 3). Make eight blocks with a red background and eight with a white background.

7 Cut two lengths of rickrack 6½" long for each block. Press a ¼" wide strip of fusible web on each piece of rickrack. Place the rickrack over the raw edges of the feedsack units. Press in place. Secure the rickrack by hand or machine.

ASSEMBLING THE QUILT

1 Using a design wall or the floor, arrange the blocks in four rows of four, alternating red and white backgrounds and rotating the strip units to form circles. Refer to Figure 4 for placement.

2 Join the blocks into rows and press, alternating the direction of the seam allowances in each row. Sew the first two rows together and the last two rows together. Then sew the two halves together and press well.

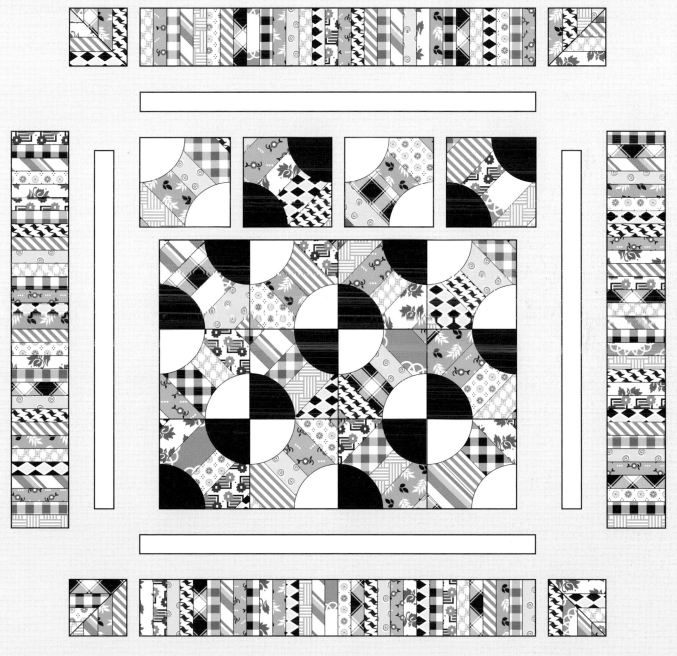

Figure 4

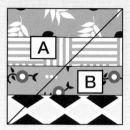
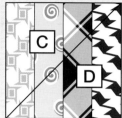

Figure 5

ADDING THE INNER BORDER

1 For the inner border, measure the length of your quilt and trim two of the 2" white border strips to match. Sew these strips to the sides of the quilt (Figure 4). Press the seam allowances toward the border.

2 Measure the width of your quilt and trim the remaining white border strip to match. Sew these to the top and bottom of the quilt. Press the seam allowances toward the border.

ADDING THE PIECED OUTER BORDER

1 Sew enough 6" feedsack strips together to make a border strip at least 32" long. Start and end with a scrap at least 2" wide. Make four of these strips. Press well.

2 Measure the length and width of your quilt, and trim the four pieced border strips to match. Sew two of the strips to the sides of the quilt. Press the seam allowances toward the inner border.

3 For each of the four border corner squares, sew several 6" feedsack strips together, then trim the pieces to 6" squares.

4 Place two of the squares with the strips running horizontally and two with the strips running vertically. Cut all four squares in half diagonally from the lower-left corner to the upper-right corner (Figure 5).

5 To make the blocks appear mitered, sew a D triangle to an A triangle and a B triangle to a C triangle (Figure 6). Press well and trim each block to 5" squares to complete the corner squares.

Figure 6

6 Sew one corner square to each end of the remaining two border strips, making sure the diagonal seams in the squares are angled toward the outside corners (Figure 7).

7 Sew one pieced border with corner squares to the top of the quilt and one to the bottom.

8 Beginning at the bottom of the quilt, securely pin or fuse the large red rickrack so it runs down the middle of the white inner border (Figure 8). Ease it around the corners and join the ends. Secure the rickrack by hand or machine.

Figure 7

Figure 8

TRY THIS!

If you don't have four continuous yards of rickrack, piece it by matching the "bumps" and taking a small seam. Press the seam allowances open and trim them so they are not visible from the top of the rickrack

Figure 9

Figure 10

Figure 11

ADDING THE APPLIQUÉ

1 On the paper side of the fusible web, trace five large blossoms, five daisies, four large half blossoms, four small half blossoms, nine centers and twenty-eight leaves from the enlarged patterns on page 124. Cut the web outlines (Figure 9).

2 Press the web outlines on the wrong sides of the appropriate fabrics, following the web manufacturer's directions. Cut each piece on the drawn line and remove the paper backing.

3 Working at the ironing board, center a large blossom with a daisy, a center and four leaves in each full circle. Refer to the picture on page 61 for placement. When you are satisfied with the arrrangement, fuse these in place (Figure 10).

4 Arrange a large half blossom, a small half blossom and a center (cut in half) in each half circle. Press these in place. Secure the appliqué pieces by hand or machine (Figure 11).

QUILTING AND FINISHING

1 Layer the top, batting and backing together to make a quilt sandwich. Quilt the layers.

2 From the binding fabric, cut five strips 2¼" wide, selvage to selvage. Sew the strips together as described on page 10 to make double fold binding. Apply the binding and add a label to finish the quilt.

About the Author

Glenna has been quilting for almost 30 years. In 2003 she opened a retail website to sell vintage quilt-related items, particularly feedsacks. From there, Glenna expanded into quilt design and publishing patterns, designing feedsack-inspired fabrics and writing a book on feedsacks called *Sugar Sack Quilts*. Glenna and her husband, Bill, are traveling more for pleasure than work these days.

Visit Glenna's website at www.hollyhockquilts.com and her blog at www.glennasgabfest.blogspot.com.

GLOWING STARS

from ¡Caliente Quilts!
by Priscilla Bianchi

Sift through your scrap bag and find all of those plaids and stripes you thought you'd never be able to use. Paired with bright tone-on-tones, neutrals and dark plaids come to life and really glow. And don't let the hexagons intimidate you—this quilt goes together without sewing inset seams!

Glowing Stars
Finished quilt: 52½" × 57"
Pieced by Priscilla Bianchi.
Quilted by Christine's Custom Quilts.

MATERIALS AND CUTTING LIST

MATERIAL	YARDAGE	CUTS	FOR
17 tone-on-tone prints	⅜ yd. each	From each, cut two 3" strips	Star blocks, 2nd Border
17 striped or plaid fabrics	⅜ yd. each	From each, cut two 3" strips.	Star blocks, 2nd Border
Dark blue fabric	¾ yd.	Cut six 2" strips. Cut two 4" strips; subcut into: • twenty-eight Template B triangles	1st Border
Binding fabric	½ yd.	n/a	Binding
Backing fabric	3¾ yds.	n/a	Backing
Batting	56" x 62"	n/a	Batting

ADDITIONAL SUPPLIES

Glowing Stars templates A & B on page 125

Figure 1

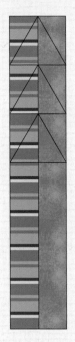

Figure 2

BEGINNING CONSTRUCTION

1 Pair up one tone-on-tone strip with a striped fabric strip. With strips right sides together, sew together lengthwise. Make a second strip set with the same tone-on-tone and stripe fabric (Figure 1). Repeat with the sixteen remaining tone-on-tone and striped fabrics. There will be a total of thirty-two strip sets, two of each fabric combination.

2 With the striped fabric on the left and the tone-on-tone on the right, place the center line of Template A on the strip set seam (Figure 2). Cut nine of Template A from each strip set.

3 Cut one strip 2¾" wide of each tone-on-tone and striped/plaid fabric. Cut each strip into thirteen squares 2¾" x 2¾" (more than needed).

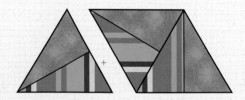

Figure 3

CONSTRUCTING THE STARS

1 Sew the Template A star points together as illustrated (Figure 3).

2 Make six half star units of each color grouping. Do not sew the half star units together.

CONSTRUCTING THE QUILT

1 Assemble the body of the quilt using the ninety-eight half star units for a total of forty-six complete stars and six half stars. Lay out all of the half star units and the Template B background triangles in horizontal rows.

2 Ensure that the two half star units of the same color will form a complete star when rows are sewn together. Arrange the different colored stars until you are pleased with the arrangement.

3 Sew together in horizontal rows (Figure 4). There will be a total of fourteen rows.

4 Sew the rows together to make your quilt center.

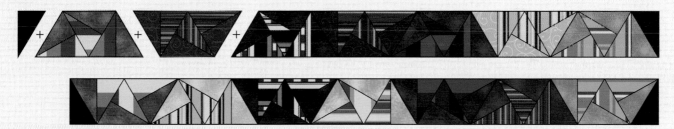

Figure 4

CONSTRUCTING THE BORDERS

1st Border

1 Cut one of the 2" wide dark blue border strips in half width-wise to make two 2" x 21" strips.

2 Sew a 2" x 21" strip end-to-end to a 2" x 42" strip. Repeat to make two long strips. Cut each to fit the width of the quilt, and sew to the top and bottom of the quilt.

3 Repeat steps 1 and 2 for the sides of the quilt. Cut to the length of the quilt and sew to the sides.

2nd Border

1 Using your choice of colors, sew enough 2½" squares together to measure the width of the quilt. Make two. If the strips are too long, trim to fit and sew to the top and bottom of the quilt.

2 Repeat step 1 for the sides of the quilt. Cut to fit the length of the quilt and sew to the sides.

3 Layer, quilt and bind.

About the Author

Guatemalan native, Priscilla Bianchi, quilt artist, designer and international teacher, represents a unique personality in today's fiber arts world. Her one-of-a-kind art quilts combine the richness and ethnic appeal of Maya Guatemalan hand-woven textiles, colors, patterns and symbolism with American quilt making, giving life to a myriad of designs that are original, fresh and innovative. Priscilla's original artwork is exhibited internationally and has been acquired by the Museum of Arts & Design in New York City and many private collectors. She designs fabric collections for Robert Kaufman in California. She teaches and lectures around the world, guides textile tours to Guatemala and operates her Maya textile export business from her hometown in Guatemala City.

Learn more about her innovative work, her many exhibitions, publications and fabric lines at www.priscillabianchi.com.

FEEDSACK PATCHES QUILT

from Granny Quilt Décor
by Darlene Zimmerman

The beautiful prints and colors of feedsacks are almost irresistible to quilters of all generations. This quilt brings together little bits of many different prints into one harmonious quilt. Try this with feedsacks, reproduction fabrics, or with any kind of special scrap collection you may have, like Civil War prints or batiks.

Feedsack Patches Quilt
Finished quilt: 38" × 48"
Pieced by Darlene Zimmerman.
Hand quilted by Pam Kienholz.

MATERIALS AND CUTTING LIST

MATERIAL	YARDAGE	CUTS	FOR
Various reproduction feedsack or other fabrics	48 6" squares	**NOTE: SEE CUTTING DIAGRAM BELOW.** From each square, cut one 2" × 6" strip. Set strip aside. Subcut remainder into one 4" square and two 2" squares.	Patches, Pieced border, Outer border
Green solid fabric	1⅓ yds.	Cut six 4" strips; subcut into: • 110—2"× 4" rectangles. Cut four 2" strips and set aside. Cut five 2¼" strips and set aside.	Sashing, Outer border, Binding
Backing fabric	45" x 55"	n/a	Backing
Batting	45" x 55"	n/a	Batting

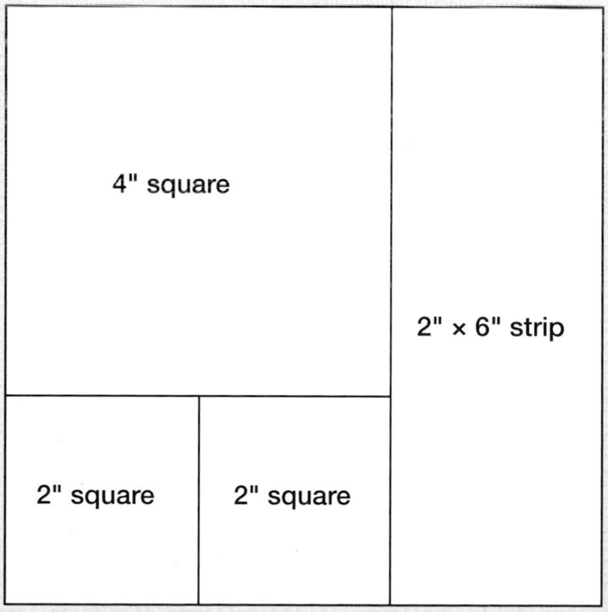

Cutting Diagram

ASSEMBLING THE QUILT CENTER

1 Join six 4" feedsack squares with seven green sashing strips to make a row. Make eight rows. Press seams toward the sashing pieces (Figure 1).

2 Join seven 2" feedsack squares and six sashing strips to make a sashing row. Make nine sashing rows. Press seams toward the sashing pieces (Figure 2).

3 Join the rows of feedsack squares and the rows of sashing, matching and pinning at seam intersections. Press the seams toward the sashing rows.

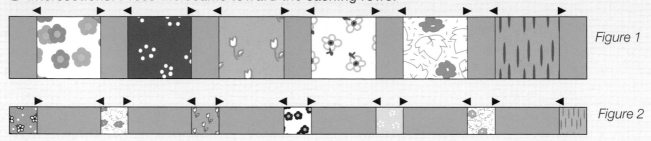

Figure 1

Figure 2

ASSEMBLE THE BORDERS

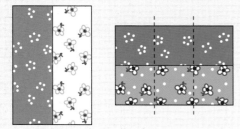

Figure 3   *Figure 4*

1 Join the 2" x 6" strips of feedsack along the long edges in pairs. Press the seam to one side (Figure 3). Make twenty-four pairs.

2 Cut each of the feedsack units into three 2" x 3½" units (Figure 4). Make seventy-two units.

3 Join ten units and one square to make the top border. Repeat for the bottom border (Figure 5).

Figure 5

4 Sew the pieced borders to the top and bottom of the quilt. Note that only the end square and the square in the center of the border will match up with the seams in the center of the quilt top. Press the border seams all one direction, unless alternating with another seam. Press the border seam toward the quilt center.

5 Join fifteen units to make the side borders. Make two. Do not press until after sewing. Sew to the sides of the quilt and press toward the quilt center.

6 Sew 2" feedsack squares to both ends of the side borders. Sew the side borders to the quilt. Press the seams toward the borders just added.

FINISHING THE QUILT

1 Mark any quilting design on the top of the quilt.

2 Layer, baste and bind. The quilt shown was hand-quilted with an orange peel design in the large feedsack squares and a leaf design in the green solid sashings and borders.

3 Sign and date your vintage/new project!

About the Author

Darlene Zimmerman lives in rural Minnesota, is married and mother of four children and grandmother to three. Her quilt career began by designing tools for EZ Quilting, and later she branched into publishing quilt books and patterns. She has published seven books with Krause Publications since 2001: *Quick Quilted Miniatures, Granny Quilts, Granny Quilt Décor, Fat Quarter Small Quilts, The Quilter's Edge, The Complete Guide to Quilting* and *Quilts from Lavender Hill Farm.*

She frequently has articles and patterns published in quilt magazines, and has also been self-publishing for her own company, Needlings, Inc. She has been noted for her 30s fabric designs for the past 14 years—first with Chanteclaire Fabrics and more recently with Robert Kaufman Fabrics.

Visit Darlene at www.feedsacklady.com.

PINEAPPLE SURPRISE

from Jelly Roll Quilts
by Pam and Nicky Lintott

What color are you always drawn to in the fabric store—red, aqua, violet? Chances are, your scrap pile has a lot of pieces that are your favorite color, as well as a lot of neutrals. Pull these pieces out to make this elegant and easy quilt. You can also use a jelly roll if your scrap supply is running a little low!

Pineapple Surprise
Finished quilt: 54" × 66"
Pieced by Pam and
Nicky Lintott.
Longarm quilted by
The Quilt Room.

MATERIALS AND CUTTING LIST

MATERIAL	YARDAGE	CUTS	FOR
Red fabric	1 jelly roll or forty 2½" wide strips	Subcut each strip into: • one 2½" x 4½" rectangle • two 2½" x 8½" rectangles • one 2½" x 12½" rectangle	Blocks
Neutral fabric	59"	Cut twelve 4½" strips; subcut into: • 100—4½" squares	Blocks
Border fabric (neutral)	23½"	Cut six 3½" x WOF strips.	Border
Binding fabric (red)	20"	Cut seven 2½" x WOF strips.	Binding
Backing	60" x 72"	n/a	Backing
Batting	60" x 72"	n/a	Batting

Figure 1

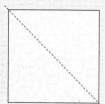

Figure 2

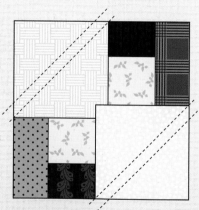

Figure 3

SEWING YOUR BLOCKS

1 Choose two 4½" rectangles and sew to top and bottom of a square. Press seams to rectangles. Choose two 8½" rectangles and sew to either side. Press seams to red rectangles (Figure 1). Choose different fabrics for a scrappy effect.

2 Take two neutral squares and draw a diagonal line from corner to corner on the reverse (Figure 2). This is your stitching guide. Place the squares on two opposite corners of your block and stitch on the marked line (Figure 3).

3 When you have stitched along the diagonal to join the corner squares to the block, stitch another line parallel using a generous ¼" seam allowance (Figure 3). You can then cut off the excess fabric by carefully cutting between the parallel lines.

4 You now have two ready-sewn half-square 'bonus' triangles to use in another scrap quilt (Figure 4).

5 Press the corners of the block open (Figure 5).

Figure 4

Figure 5

6 Choose two 8½" rectangles and sew to the top and bottom of the block. Press seams to rectangles. Then choose two 12½" rectangles and sew to either side. Press seams to rectangles (Figure 6).

7 Take two more squares and draw a diagonal line from corner to corner on the reverse as before. Place them on the two opposite corners and stitch on the marked line. Stitch the parallel line as before (Figure 7).

8 When you cut between the two lines you will have created two more bonus triangles (Figure 8).

9 Now you've got the idea, you can start chain-piecing to speed up the sewing. You need twenty blocks, as shown in Figure 9.

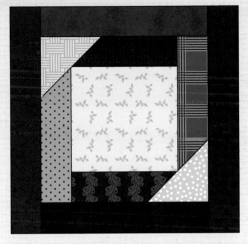

Figure 6

Figure 7

Figure 8

Figure 9

TRY THIS!

The blade on your rotary cutter will eventually become dull. If you notice that it takes more pressure to cut, or if it misses a few threads when cutting, then it is time to change the blade. You will be amazed at the difference it makes. Take care when changing the blade, carefully laying out the pieces in the correct order so you know exactly how to put them back together.

Figure 10

SEWING YOUR BLOCKS TOGETHER

Referring to Figure 10, join the blocks together, four across and five down.

FINISHING THE QUILT

1 Join your six 3½" wide border strips into one continuous length.

2 Determine the vertical measurement from top to bottom through the center of your quilt top. Cut two side border strips to this measurement. Placing right sides together, stitch quilt and side borders together, easing the quilt side to fit where necessary.

3 Determine the horizontal measurement from side to side across the center of the quilt top. Cut two top and bottom border strips to this measurement and add to the quilt top in the same manner as before. Your quilt top is now complete.

4 Quilt as desired and bind to finish.

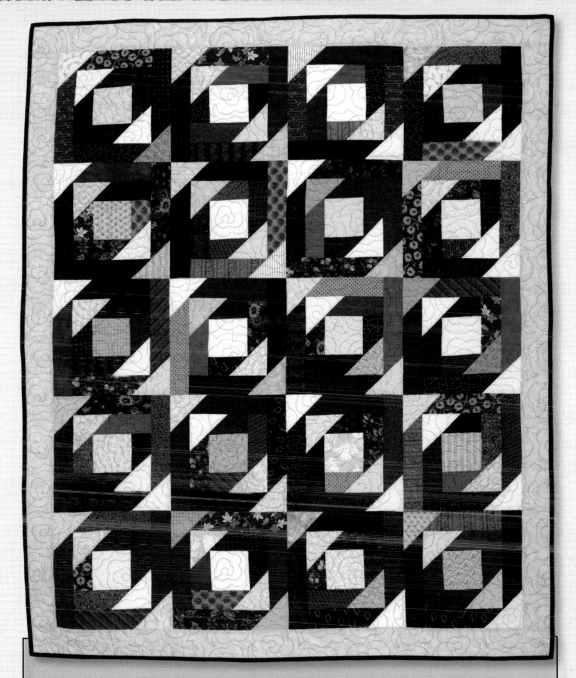

About the Authors

Pam Lintott started The Quilt Room in Dorking, England back in 1981, which she now runs with her daughter, Nicky. Big celebrations are planned as their 30th anniversary approaches! Pam and Nicky have now written four books, including their best-seller *Jelly Roll Quilts*. Their other titles include *Layer Cake, Jelly Roll and Charm Quilts, Jelly Roll Challenge* and *Two From One Jelly Roll Quilts*.

Visit Pam and Nicky at www.quiltroom.co.uk and at their blog (which includes the latest patchwork and quilting information) at www.quiltroom.typepad.co.uk.

TRIANGLE DYNAMICS

from Scrap Quilt Sensation
by Katharine Guerrier

This show-stopping quilt is made with only scraps and half-square triangle units. Mix-and-match lights and darks, arrange the triangles into an array of designs and "Voila!" Put your unique spin on this quilt by twisting and turning the blocks any way you like to create your own special work of art.

Triangle Dynamics
Finished quilt: 51" × 51"
Pieced and quilted by Katharine Guerrier.

MATERIALS AND CUTTING LIST

NOTE: FOR THE BASIC UNITS, ANY SCRAPS LARGER THAN A 4" SQUARE WILL WORK.
FOR THE MINI BLOCKS, THE LARGEST SQUARE REQUIRED IS 4½".

MATERIAL	YARDAGE	FOR
Cotton fabric scraps	5½ yds. total	Blocks
Backing fabric	59" x 59"	Backing
Binding fabric	1 yd.	Binding
Batting	59" x 59"	Batting

TRY THIS!

When buying fabrics there always seems to be more appealing dark fabrics than light ones. This quilt reflects my collection before I started making an effort to acquire a bigger range of light fabrics, as my quilts seemed to be getting increasingly darker. Without the lime green, yellow and pink in the mini blocks, the darker fabrics would dominate. I have made several versions of this pattern in a number of different sizes. The possible variations seem to be endless as no two turn out the same. I used patterned fabrics but you could use plains, too. When making the mini blocks, choose bright colors teamed with dark or use high-contrast dark/light pairs to make the pinwheels more visible.

Figure 1

Figure 2

ASSEMBLY

The quilt is assembled from half-square triangle units arranged in a variety of ways to create 12" blocks and from mini units, also based on half-square triangles, made up to fit into the blocks. Work in the order given to make a total of nine blocks, some including the mini units. You will need additional fabrics for the chevron border.

MAKING THE HALF-SQUARE TRIANGLE UNITS

1 From the light and dark fabrics cut 3½" squares in at least thirty-two different fabrics.

2 Place these right sides together in pairs of one light and one dark fabric. Draw a diagonal line on the wrong side of the lighter fabric. Stitch ¼" away from the line on both sides. Cut down the drawn line and open out the fabrics. You now have two half-square triangle units. Press the seams open or to one side. Trim off all the extending points from the seam allowances.

3 Make up thirty-two (or more) bi-colored squares.

MAKING THE BASIC BLOCK

One basic block is made up from sixteen half-square triangle units arranged in a block of 4 x 4.

1 Half-square triangle units can be arranged in blocks of 4 x 4 in a variety of ways to create many intriguing patterns. Refer to Figure 2 to make one or two blocks in different designs. Stars, diamonds and zigzags can all be created just by altering the orientation of the seams. You will probably discover more than are illustrated here.

2 Next make up some of the mini units as explained on pages 81-83 and make further blocks using these. Make as many different patterns as you like.

MAKING MINI UNIT A

There are three different variations of the mini blocks: A, B and C. The A block will replace four of the basic units and introduce the larger pinwheel as part of the block.

1 Choose three or more fabrics: two for the center pinwheel and one to four for the corners—the pinwheel fabrics should be light or bright and dark and the corners fairly light.

2 Cut one square 4¼" of each of the pinwheel fabrics and place these right sides together. Draw two diagonal lines across the wrong side of the lighter fabric. Stitch in a "windmill" pattern (Figure 3), sewing ¼" away from the drawn lines, from the edge of the squares to the center.

3 Cut across both diagonals. This will yield four bi-colored triangles.

4 Using the remaining fabric(s) selected for the corners, cut two squares 3⅞". Divide these into four triangles by cutting across one diagonal. Now stitch one pieced triangle to one of these corner triangles. Repeat three more times (Figure 4).

5 Stitch the resulting squares together to make the A block (Figure 4).

MAKING A BLOCK WITH UNIT A

Make a block using twelve half-square triangle units and replacing the other four with the A unit. Follow the arrangement shown in Figure 5 or use your own design.

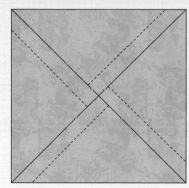

Figure 3

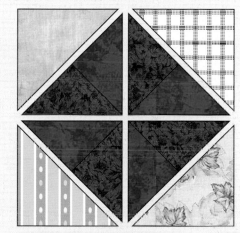

Figure 4

Figure 5

Figure 6

Figure 7

MAKING MINI UNIT B

The B block is also a pinwheel but made on a smaller scale. Like mini block A, it can be used to replace four of the half-square triangle units.

1 Choose two high-contrast fabrics in light or bright and dark combinations for the pinwheel.

2 Cut two squares $3\frac{3}{8}$" from each of the fabrics.

3 Place your squares right sides together in pairs of one light and one dark fabric and repeat the "windmill" sewing sequence as for the A block (Figure 4). Cut across the diagonal lines to create the bi-colored triangles. This time you will have eight.

4 Join these bi-colored triangles in pairs to make four quarter-square triangle units (Figure 6).

5 Stitch the quarter-square triangle units together in pairs, then join the pairs to make the pinwheel (Figure 7).

6 Cut two squares $3\frac{7}{8}$" for the corner triangles and then cut these into triangles by cutting across one diagonal. These can be all the same fabric or four different ones to add to the scrap look. Add these triangles to opposite sides of the pinwheel. Press the seams, then add the other two and press again (Figure 7).

MAKING A BLOCK WITH UNIT B

Make a block using twelve half-square triangle units and replacing the other four with the B unit. Follow the arrangement shown in Figure 8 or use your own design.

Figure 8

MAKING MINI UNIT C

This unit can replace one of the half-triangle units and can be scattered across the quilt to add jewel points. Once again, it is based on half-triangle units that can be arranged to create different effects.

1 Choose two high-contrast fabrics in light or bright and dark combinations for the unit.

2 Cut two squares $2^3/_8$" from each fabric. Place these right sides together and make half-square triangle units as explained on page 80.

3 Join the resulting four squares to create an eye-catching block, referring to Figure 9 for possible arrangements.

Figure 9

MAKING A BLOCK WITH UNIT C

Make a block using fourteen half-square triangle units and replacing the other two with C units. Follow the arrangement shown in Figure 10 or use your own design.

JOINING THE BLOCKS

When you have made a number of blocks, arrange them edge-to-edge, using a design wall, if possible. Move them around until you are satisfied with the overall effect. You will find that the individual blocks will "disappear" to make an overall pattern. My quilt has nine blocks, but you can use more or less to fulfill the size requirement of your quilt.

NOTE: THE BORDER WILL ADD 6" OR 9" TO EACH SIDE.

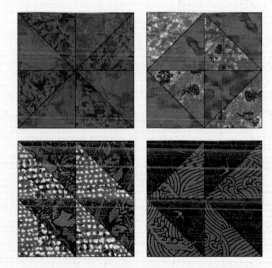

Figure 10

MAKING THE CHEVRON BORDER

The border comprises basic half-triangle blocks arranged over two or three rows in a simple chevron pattern around the edge of the quilt.

1 Make more of the basic 3" half-square triangle units. (These are 3½" including the seam allowance.)

2 Arrange these so that the light and dark triangles form a zigzag pattern around the outer edges of the quilt. Join the units together. In the quilt shown on page 85 the chevron border is two units deep on two adjacent sides and three units deep on the other two sides, as shown in Figures 11 and 12. The corners are filled with squares cut 3½". You can make the focus of the chevron light or dark. Refer to the photograph on page 85 as a guide.

3 Stitch the borders to the edges of the quilt. Press the seams.

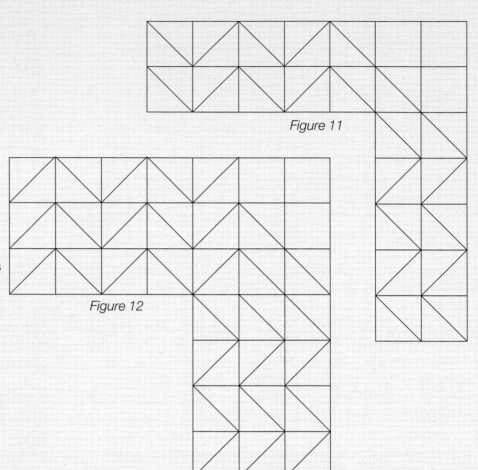

Figure 11

Figure 12

QUILTING THE LAYERS

1 Cut the batting and the backing fabric so that they are 1½" larger all round than the quilt top. Assemble the three layers of the quilt with the quilt top centered on the batting, and the backing fabric underneath. Pin and then tack (baste) horizontal and vertical grid lines about 4" apart across the entire quilt.

2 Quilt as desired by hand or machine using an appropriate quilting thread. I machine quilted in zigzag lines using invisible monofilament thread and a walking foot on the machine. I did not try to quilt in parallel lines to the seams. Instead the zigzag lines were deliberately offset to make the quilting easy and overcome the necessity of marking the quilting lines.

BINDING AND FINISHING

Cut the binding strips 2½" wide, piecing them together as necessary to make up the required length. Trim the batting and backing fabrics a scant ¼" beyond the edge of the quilt top. Press the binding in half lengthways with wrong sides facing and attach it to the quilt following the instructions on pages 10-11.

About the Author

Katharine Guerrier has been making quilts and smaller items since 1980. She studied printed textiles at Camberwell Art College, London UK. In addition to teaching the techniques to groups of enthusiastic quilters, she also writes books on the subject, the most recent entitled *Scrap Quilt Sensation,* published by David & Charles. Three books on CD, including *Patchwork Postcards* and *Pinboard Quilts,* are her latest ventures in publishing. Katharine's work has been featured in various magazines, both British and American, and she is a regular contributor to local and national quilt exhibitions. Her work draws on the traditional motifs of pieced-patchwork, developing the motifs to have a contemporary feel, and uses color as an important part of the design process. Katharine's interest in all the decorative arts provides the incentive to create textiles that are both original and collectible.

Visit Katharine at www.katharineguerrier.com.

EMBRACING TRADITION

N o matter what kind of quilter you are or what fabrics you are drawn to, we are all influenced by our quilting heritage. Take this opportunity to embrace tradition! These beautiful quilts are reminiscent of a time gone by, but they all have a hint of the quilter's unique point of view incorporated into them.

If you love traditional quilts, you will love making these next five projects and they will soon become keepsakes and heirlooms in your family.

If you've never made a traditional quilt before, use these next projects as a jumping-off point for combining your own aesthetic with a piece of your quilt history.

From **Quilts from Lavender Hill Farm**
by Darlene Zimmerman

SUNNY POPPY CLUB

from Rainy Day Appliqué
by Ursula Michael

Not only does this cheerful wall hanging immediately make you smile, it is the perfect stash-buster quilt. Dig through the fat quarters you have collected over the years to find the perfect combination of colors for the vibrant poppy appliqué. Sort through the forgotten neutrals, solids and basics in your workroom for the perfect background and borders in this sunny quilt.

Experiment with different colors, textures and prints to create a quilt that makes you smile, no matter what the weather!

Sunny Poppy Club
Finished quilt: 25½" × 21½"
Piece and quilted by
Ursula Michael.

MATERIALS AND CUTTING LIST

MATERIAL	YARDAGE	CUTS	FOR
Assorted medium red prints	Fat quarters	Cut one strip 1¼" × 84" (pieced to achieve required length).	Poppies, Border
Medium green prints	Fat quarters	See instructions on page 96.	Leaves and stems
Light yellow print or batik	½ yd.	Cut one rectangle 21" × 17".	Background
Medium green print	¼ yd.	Cut one strip 3¼" × 96" (pieced to achieve required length).	Binding
Backing fabric	27" × 23"	n/a	Backing
Batting	27" × 23"	n/a	Batting

ADDITIONAL SUPPLIES

Monofilament thread for quilting
Quilt basting spray
Fusible web
SUNNY POPPY CLUB pattern on page 126

Figure 1

TRY THIS!

Do you like a pattern, but the colors aren't right for you? Think how lovely this design would look with a dark blue background and white appliquéd poppies, or sunny yellow poppies dancing on sky blue fabric.

PIECING

1 Sew the red border strip around the light yellow background section.

2 Sew the green binding strip around the yellow/red background section (Figure 1).

ASSEMBLY

1 Prepare the appliqué shapes using your favorite fusible method.

2 Arrange the individual poppy, stem and leaf pieces on the center section.

3 Press in place.

FINISHING

1 Layer the finished top, batting and backing.

2 Apply quilt basting spray.

3 This model was quilted in a free form style to complement the poppies.

4 After quilting is complete, trim excess batting and backing.

5 Fold back the front outer border and hand sew the edges to the back side to finish.

About the Author

As a professional quilt and award winning needlework designer, Ursula Michael has combined her love of sewing, designing, fiber art and working with fabric into a fabulous career in the world of crafts. With a keen eye for color and design, easy projects and a variety of techniques, Ursula shares her whimsical art and heartfelt love of working with fabrics and thread with sewers in a variety of interests. Ursula has written three F+W Media books: *Rainy Day Appliqué*, *Whimsical Machine Embroidery*, and *Cross Stitch by the Sea*. She has designed well over 1,000 designs for cross stitch, quilting, machine embroidery, greeting cards and print media.

Visit Ursula at http://ursulamichael.com.

CHOCOLATE RASPBERRY TRUFFLE

from Quilts from Lavender Hill Farm
by Darlene Zimmerman

Some things never go out of style—like chocolate, raspberries and this beautiful basket block. Find color inspiration from your favorite sweet-treat, fabrics from a time gone by or even a handful of paint chips. This is a quilt you'll use year after year to snuggle under with a cup of hot chocolate, a decadent dessert and a good book.

Chocolate Raspberry Truffle
Finished quilt: 41" × 52"
Piece and quilted by Darlene Zimmerman.

MATERIALS AND CUTTING LIST

MATERIAL	YARDAGE	CUTS	FOR
Cream floral fabric	1¼ yds.	*Blocks*—Cut two 3½" × 42" strips; sub-cut into: • thirty-six 3½" Easy Angle triangles* *Blocks*—Cut seven 2" × 42" strips; sub-cut into: • seventy-two 2" Easy Angle triangles* • thirty-six 2" × 3½" rectangles • eighteen 2" × 2" squares *Triangles*—Cut two 4½" × 42" strips; sub-cut into: • ten 4½" × 4½" squares *Triangles*—Cut two 2½" × 42" strips; sub-cut into: • twenty-eight 2½" × 2½" squares	Block background, Setting triangles
Assorted pink prints	6 fat quarters	*Blocks*—From each fat quarter, cut one 3½" × 21" strip; sub-cut into: • two 3½" Easy Angle triangles* *Blocks*—From each fat quarter, cut one 2" × 21" strip; sub-cut into: • twelve 2" Easy Angle triangles* *Blocks*—From each fat quarter, cut two 1½" × 21" strips; sub-cut into: • two 1½" × 8½" rectangles • two 1½" × 6½" rectangles *Triangles*—From each fat quarter, cut two 2" × 21" strips; sub-cut into: • ten Companion Angle triangles**	Blocks/Sashing, Setting triangles
Assorted brown prints	3 fat quarters	From each fat quarter: Cut one 3½" × 21" strip; sub-cut into: • two 3½" Easy Angle triangles* Cut one 2" × 21" strip; sub-cut into: • twelve 2" Easy Angle triangles* Cut seven 1½" × 21" strips; sub-cut into: • eight 1½" × 8½" rectangles • eight 1½" × 6½" rectangles	Blocks/Sashing
Brown print	⅔ yd.	Cut five 4" × 42" strips.	Border
Pink print	⅜ yd.	Cut five 2¼" × 42" strips.	Binding
Backing fabric	2⅔ yd.	n/a	Backing
Batting	Crib size	n/a	Batting

ADDITIONAL SUPPLIES

Easy Angle tool (*optional*)
Companion Angle tool (*optional*)

NOTE: SEE PAGE 15 FOR MORE INSTRUCTIONS ON USING THESE TOOLS.

* IF NOT USING EASY ANGLE, CUT 3⅞" AND 2⅜" SQUARES, RESPECTIVELY. CUT ONCE ON THE DIAGONAL.

**IF NOT USING COMPANION ANGLE, CUT THREE 4¼" × 4¼" SQUARES FROM EACH FABRIC. CUT THE SQUARES TWICE ON THE DIAGONAL TO YIELD TWELVE TRIANGLES. YOU WILL HAVE SOME LEFT OVER.

Figure 1

ASSEMBLING THE BASKET BLOCKS

1 Match either a large or small background triangle right sides together with either a pink or brown triangle. From each fabric sew eight matching small and two matching large triangle squares together. Press toward the darker fabric. Trim the dog-ears (Figure 1). (There will be some small brown and pink triangles left over for step 6.)

2 Sew matching small triangle squares together in A and B pairs as shown (Figure 2). Press.

3 Sew the A sets of triangle squares from step 2 to the left side of the matching large triangle squares (Figure 3). Press. Repeat for each of the eighteen basket blocks.

4 Sew a background square to the left side of the B-triangle squares from step 2 (Figure 4). Press towards the square. Repeat for each of the B-triangle squares.

5 Sew the step 4 units to the top of the step 3 units (Figure 5). Press.

6 Sew a matching pair of small pink or brown triangles to the 2" × 3½" background rectangles as shown. Make two As and Bs of each print (Figure 6). Trim the dog-ears. Press.

A   B

Figure 2

Figure 3

Figure 4

Figure 5

A   B

Figure 6

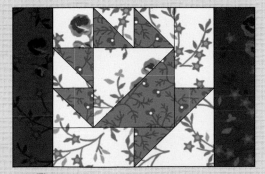

Figure 7   Figure 8

7 Sew the step 6 units to adjacent sides of the basket blocks (Figure 7). Trim dog-ears. Press.

8 Sew a background triangle to the bottom of the block (Figure 8). Press. At this point the blocks should measure 6½" × 6½".

9 Make twelve pink and six brown basket blocks.

NOTE: IF YOUR BLOCKS MEASURE LESS THAN 6½" × 6½", TRIM THE SASHING STRIPS IN THE NEXT TWO STEPS TO FIT YOUR BLOCKS.

SASHING THE BLOCKS

1 Using two different 1½" × 6½" pink sashings, sew them to opposite sides of the brown basket blocks (Figure 9). Press toward the sashing.

2 Using different 1½" × 8½" pink sashings, sew to the remaining sides of the brown basket blocks (Figure 10). Press toward the sashing.

3 Using different 1½" × 6½" brown sashings, sew to opposite sides of the pink basket blocks (Figure 11). Press toward the sashing.

NOTE: THE SASHINGS ARE SEWN ON OPPOSITE SIDES FROM THE BROWN BASKET BLOCKS.

4 Using different 1½" × 8½" brown sashings, sew to the remaining sides of the pink basket blocks (Figure 12). Press toward the sashing.

Figure 9

Figure 10

Figure 11   Figure 12

Figure 13

Figure 14

ASSEMBLING THE SETTING TRIANGLES

1 Sew a pink triangle to the right side of the 2½" × 2½" background square (Figure 13). Press toward the triangle. Repeat for each of the background squares.

2 Sew a different pink triangle to the left side of the step 1 units (Figure 14). Press toward the triangles. (You will have some triangles left over.)

3 Sew a step 2 unit to the right side of a 4½" × 4½" background square (Figure 15). Repeat to make a total of ten units. Press toward the background square.

4 Sew a step 2 unit to the left side of the step 3 unit (Figure 16). Press. Repeat to make a total of ten units.

5 Using two of the step 2 units, sew together to make a corner triangle (Figure 17). Repeat to make four corner triangles. Press the seam open.

Figure 15

Figure 16

Figure 17

ASSEMBLING THE QUILT TOP

1 Arrange the setting triangles and the pink and brown blocks in diagonal rows (Figure 18). Sew the blocks together in rows. Press the seams toward the brown sashing.

2 Sew the rows together, pinning and matching seam allowances. Press the row seams all one direction.

3 Trim the edges even, if necessary, leaving at least ¼" seam allowance from the corners of the brown sashing.

ADDING THE BORDERS

1 Measure the quilt width through the center of the quilt. Trim two 4" × 42" brown borders to this length. Sew to the top and bottom of the quilt, pressing the seams toward the borders. See page 9 for more instruction on adding borders.

2 Measure the quilt length through the center of the quilt. Diagonally piece the remaining three border strips, then trim two borders the length of the quilt. Sew to the sides of the quilt, pressing the seams toward the borders just added.

Figure 18

FINISHING THE QUILT

1 Piece the backing, and trim the excess, allowing at least 2" extra on all sides of the quilt top. Trim the batting to the same size as the backing. Layer the backing wrong side up, then the batting, and lastly the quilt top, right side up. Baste.

2 Quilt as desired. The quilt shown was machine-quilted in the ditch around each of the blocks and the frames. Hand-quilting was added inside the blocks. A four-petaled flower was quilted in the large setting triangles and a design was quilted in the border.

3 Before binding, hand-baste a scant ¼" from the edge of the quilt to hold the layers together and prevent shifting while the binding is being sewn on.

BINDING

1 Prepare the binding by sewing together the pink 2¼" × 42" binding lengths with diagonal seams pressed open. Press the binding in half the long way, with the right side out. (See page 10 for more instruction on preparing binding.)

2 Sew the binding to the quilt with a ¼" seam, mitering the corners. (See page 11 for mitering corners.)

3 Join the binding ends with a "Perfect Fit" ending. (See pages 12–13 for more instruction on ending the binding.)

4 Sign your quilt and enjoy!

About the Author

Darlene Zimmerman lives in rural Minnesota, is married and mother of four children and grandmother to three. Her quilt career began by designing tools for EZ Quilting, and later she branched into publishing quilt books and patterns. She has published seven books with Krause Publications since 2001: *Quick Quilted Miniatures, Granny Quilts, Granny Quilts Décor!, Fat Quarter Small Quilts, The Quilter's Edge, The Complete Guide to Quilting* and *Quilts from Lavender Hill Farm*. She frequently has articles and patterns published in quilt magazines, and has also been self-publishing for her own company, Needlings, Inc. She is also noted for her 30s fabric designs.

Visit Darlene at www.feedsacklady.com.

DATE NIGHT TRIPPER

from Traditional Quilts with a Twist
by Maggie Ball

Designing with traditional blocks in unconventional layouts and colors is always rewarding and exciting. Embrace your quilting heritage with these pieced blocks, but add your own unique style by using bold fabrics and creating new patterns. This amazing quilt will inspire you to put a new twist on traditional blocks!

NEW SKILLS!

Learn to piece sawtooth star and bowtie blocks while you make this quilt.

Date Night Tripper
Finished quilt: 27" × 27"
Pieced and quilted by Maggie Ball.

MATERIALS AND CUTTING LIST

NOTE: UNLESS OTHERWISE INDICATED, ALL STRIPS ARE CUT ACROSS THE FULL WIDTH OF THE FABRIC, SELVAGE TO SELVAGE (40").

MATERIAL	YARDAGE	CUTS	FOR
Yellow fabric	¼ yd.	*Star points*—Cut three 1¼" strips; sub-cut into: • seventy-two 1¼" squares *Star centers*—Cut nine 2" squares.	Sawtooth star blocks
Blue fabric	½ yd.	*Stars*—Cut three 1¼" strips; sub-cut into: • thirty-six 1¼" × 2" rectangles (side rectangles) • thirty-six 1¼" squares (corner squares) *Nine-patches*—Cut three 1½" strips *Bowties*—Cut two 2" strips; sub-cut into: • thirty-two 2" squares *Four-patches*—Cut one 2" strip.	Sawtooth star blocks, Nine-patches, Bowties, Four-patches
Red fabric	⅓ yd.	*Nine-patches*—Cut two 1½" strips. *Four patches*—Cut one 2" × 20" stip. *Borders*—Cut two 1¼" × 21½" strips. *Borders*—Cut two 1¼" × 23" strips.	Nine-patches, Four-patches, Borders
Black fabric	¾ yd.	*Nine-patches*—Cut two 1½" strips. *Bowties*—Cut two 2" strips; sub-cut into: • thirty-two 2" squares *Bowties (corner triangles)*—Cut one 1¼" strip; sub-cut into: • thirty-two 1¼" squares *Four-patches*—Cut one 2" × 20" strip. *Borders*—Cut two 2½" × 23" strips. *Borders*—Cut two 2½" × 27" strips.	Nine-patches, Bowties, Four-patches, Borders
Binding fabric (black)	¼ yd.	Cut three 2½" strips.	Binding
Backing fabric	30" × 30"	n/a	Backing
Batting	30" × 30"	n/a	Batting

ADDITIONAL SUPPLIES

Fine mechanical pencil (0.5 mm lead)

Figure 1

PIECING THE SAWTOOTH STAR BLOCKS

1 Make thirty-six corner-square triangles for the star points using the yellow 1¼" squares and the blue 1¼" × 2" rectangles. Mark the yellow squares on the wrong side with a diagonal line, corner to corner, using a fine mechanical pencil. Sew along the marked line to attach them to the blue rectangles. Once the seam is stitched, trim away the excess seam allowance, and then press the seam allowance toward the blue fabric (Figure 1) to complete these flying geese units.

2 Sew two of the flying geese units to opposite sides of a yellow center square; press the seams toward the center square. Join the blue corner squares to each end of the remaining two corner-square triangle units; press the seams toward the corners. Stitch the side units onto the center sections and press the seams toward the center sections (Figure 2).

3 Make nine sawtooth star blocks.

Figure 2

PIECING THE NINE-PATCH BLOCKS

1 Cut the 1½" full-width strips into smaller sections according to the number of three-square units needed (Figure 3), plus a couple of inches to allow for errors: 26" for sixteen units, one full-width plus 11" for thirty-two units.

2 Strip-piece the 1½" strips, press the seams away from the blue. Sub-cut them 1½" to create the required three-square units (Figure 4).

3 Join these units to construct sixteen nine-patch blocks (Figure 5).

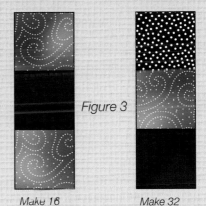

Figure 3

Make 16   Make 32

Figure 4

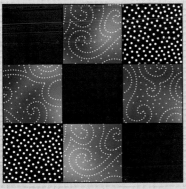

Make 8

Figure 5

Make 8

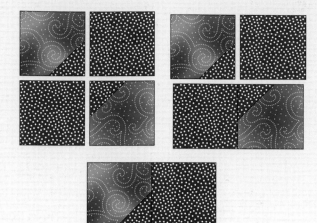

Figure 6

PIECING THE BOWTIE BLOCKS

1 Use the corner-square triangle method (see "Piecing the Sawtooth Star Blocks") to make the small black corner triangle squares in one corner of each of the blue squares. Press the seams away from the triangles.

2 Lay out the corner-square triangle units and the black 2" squares in the bowtie format and join them in pairs (Figure 6). Press the seams toward the black fabric.

3 Assemble the pairs of squares and press the final seam open. Make sixteen bowtie blocks.

PIECING THE FOUR-PATCH BLOCKS

1 Cut the full-width blue strip in half.

2 Stitch one half of the blue strip to the red 2" × 20" strip and the other half to the black 2" × 20" strip. Press the seams away from the blue fabric.

3 Sub-cut the strips 2" (eight of each type) and pair them together to make the four-patches (Figure 7). Construct eight four-patch blocks.

ASSEMBLING THE QUILT

1 Lay out the forty-nine blocks in the desired configuration and piece them in rows. Press the seams so that the seam allowances on adjacent rows will nest in opposing directions. Assemble the rows.

2 Add the 21½" inner borders to the sides and the 23" borders to the top and bottom. Repeat to add the 23" outer borders to the sides and the 27" outer borders to the top and bottom. Alternatively, miter the corners of the borders (see page 116).

3 Lay the quilt back flat, wrong side up on a firm surface. Place the batting on top of the backing and smooth out. Layer the quilt top, right-side up, over the batting. Baste the layers and quilt as desired. The sample quilt features a diagonal grid of serpentine stitches.

4 Bind the quilt (see pages 10–11).

Figure 7

About the Author

Maggie Ball began quilting in 1986 and enjoys creating her own designs from elements of traditional patterns. Her award-winning quilts have been exhibited nationally and overseas. Teaching quilting is a natural extension of her passion and she finds it rewarding. Her teaching experience is extensive in the USA, and beyond to the UK and Mongolia, as well as quilting with over 800 children in local schools. Maggie's books, *Creative Quilting with Kids* and *Patchwork and Quilting with Kids,* aim to encourage adults to pass on the quilting tradition to the next generation. *Traditional Quilts with a Twist* contains new patterns derived from traditional blocks. Her most recent book, *Bargello Quilts with a Twist*, features quilts made from her original, easy to construct, 16-piece bargello block.

For more information on the Mongolian project and the classes and lectures Maggie offers, visit her website at www.dragonflyquilts.com.

CONFETTI

from Granny Quilts
by Darlene Zimmerman

It's the little details that make any handmade item special, like the scalloped border on this quilt. You'll be surprised how quickly and easily this vibrant little quilt comes togther. This will truly become an heirloom quilt for generations to treasure!

Confetti

Finished Quilt: 51" × 60"
Vintage top.
Hand quilted by
Darlene Zimmerman.

MATERIALS AND CUTTING LIST

MATERIAL	YARDAGE	CUTS	FOR
White fabric	2¼ yds.	Cut fifteen 5" strips; sub-cut into: • 120—5" squares	Fan blocks
Red solid fabric	2 yds.	Cut six 1½" strips; sub-cut into: • 110—1½" squares Cut fourteen 1¾" strips.	Fan blocks, Borders, Binding
Bright yellow solid fabric	⅔ yd.	Cut five 2" strips; sub-cut into: • 100—2" squares Cut seven 1" strips.	Fan blocks, Borders
Variety of prints	1½ yds. total	Cut 2½" strips, sub-cut into: • 500 wedges using the template on page 118	Fan blocks
Backing fabric	3¼ yds.	n/a	Backing
Batting	55" × 65"	n/a	Batting

ADDITIONAL SUPPLIES

Large square ruler
Freezer paper
Companion Angle (*optional*)
Confetti templates on page 118

TRY THIS!

For fans with folded points, try using an Easy Dresden tool.

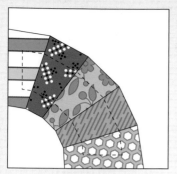

Figure 1

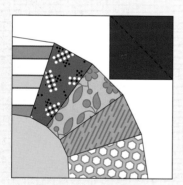

Figure 2

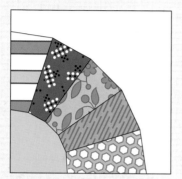

Figure 3

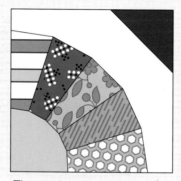

Figure 4

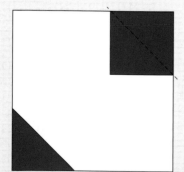

Figure 5

MAKING THE BLOCKS

1 Sew five wedges together to make a fan. Turn under the top edge ¼" and press. Baste in place in the corner of a white square (Figure 1). Repeat to make 100 fan blocks.

2 Stitch the top curve of the fans in place by hand using a neutral thread and blind hem stitch. Or, use a tiny zigzag or blind hem stitch for machine appliqué. Other options include buttonhole stitching by hand or machine with black thread or with black pearl cotton (#8 for hand stitching), or machine stitch rickrack over the finished top edge.

3 Make freezer paper templates for the fan base from the template given on page 118. Iron the template to the wrong side of the yellow squares, fitting the corner of the template into the corner of the square. Add a scant ¼" seam allowance to the curved edge only as you are cutting out the shapes. Finger press or, with a warm iron, press the curved edge around the freezer paper template. Stitch the fan base in place by hand or machine. Remove the freezer paper before or after stitching. Remove the basting thread.

4 Trim away some of the white background behind the fan and the fan base. This will make it easier to needle for hand quilting. If machine quilting, you can leave the extra fabric behind the fans for added stability.

5 On the wrong side of each red square, mark a diagonal line. On the corner opposite of the fan base, place a red square and sew on the marked line (Figure 3). Trim off the excess fabric, leaving a ¼" seam allowance. Press the seam toward the red triangle (Figure 4). Repeat for each of the blocks.

6 On the remaining twenty plain white blocks, add a red square in opposite corners (Figure 5).

ASSEMBLING THE QUILT

1 For the top and bottom A rows, sew together five fan blocks alternated with five plain blocks. Press toward the plain blocks (Figure 6). Make two rows like this.

Figure 6
Make 2

2 Make ten B rows as shown (Figure 7). Press seams away from even numbered blocks.

Figure 7
Make 10

3 Sew the rows together referring to Figure 8. Begin with the top A row, then a B row, followed by a B row reversed. Repeat B and B reversed rows and end with an A row reversed. Press the seam allowances in one direction.

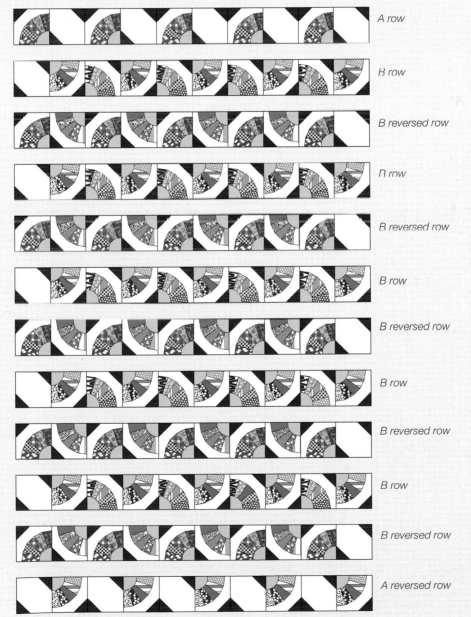

A row

B row

B reversed row

B row

B reversed row

B row

B reversed row

B row

B reversed row

B row

B reversed row

A reversed row

Figure 8

ADDING BORDERS WITH MITERED CORNERS

1 Piece the borders together first—red-yellow-red—in extra-long border lengths.

2 Sew the borders to the quilt, beginning and ending ¼" in from each corner. Backstitch at each end. Press the seam allowances toward the quilt.

3 Fold the quilt on the diagonal, right sides together, matching raw edges with the borders extending outward.

4 Lay a Companion Angle (or a ruler) on your quilt with the longest edge on the diagonal fold, and the side of the tool aligned with the raw edges of the borders (Figure 9). Draw a line from the diagonal fold to the edge of the borders.

5 Pin the borders together along this line. Stitch on the line, backstitching at the inside corner.

6 Check the seam on the right side. If it is properly sewn, trim the seam to ¼" and press open. Repeat on all four corners.

Figure 9

FINISHING THE QUILT

1 Layer, baste and quilt.

2 Before binding, mark the notch (see pattern on page 118) at the edges directly above the point where the quilt top is notched. Hand or machine baste (using a walking foot) a scant ¼" from the edge of the quilt, and following the marked notches. Do not trim this edge yet!

3 Make bias binding using strips 1¼" wide cut from remaining red solid fabric. Join the strips with diagonal seams and press open. Press the beginning edge under ¼".

4 With right sides together and the raw edge of the binding aligned with the marked border, begin stitching a ¼" seam at the top of the scallop. Stitch to the base of the V, stop with needle down, lift the presser foot, pivot the quilt and binding, and sew out of the V (Figure 10). Continue around the quilt in this manner. Overlap the beinning edge by 1" and trim off at an angle.

5 Trim the seam allowance even with the edge of the binding. Turn the binding to the back side, turn under ¼" and stitch down by hand, covering the stitching line. The inside corners will just fold over upon themselves automatically.

6 Sign and date your cheerful masterpiece!

Figure 10

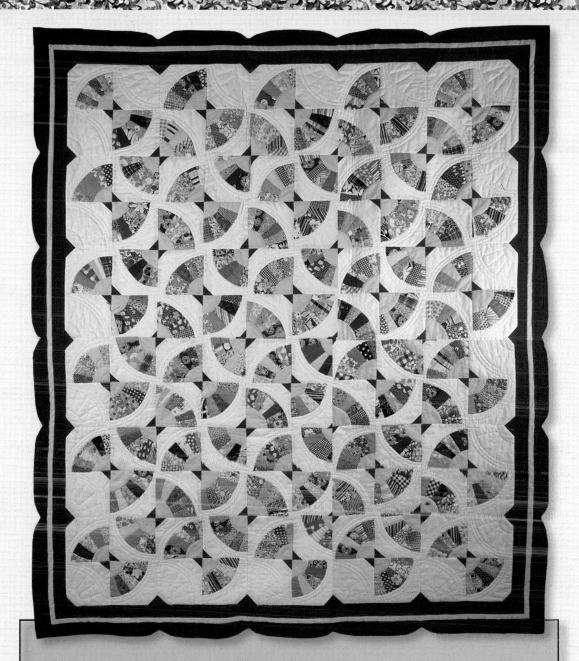

About the Author

Darlene Zimmerman lives in rural Minnesota, is married and mother of four children and grandmother to three. Her quilt career began by designing tools for EZ Quilting, and later she branched into publishing quilt books and patterns. She has published seven books with Krause Publications since 2001: *Quick Quilted Miniatures, Granny Quilts, Granny Quilts Décor!, Fat Quarter Small Quilts, The Quilter's Edge, The Complete Guide to Quilting* and *Quilts from Lavender Hill Farm*.

She frequently has articles and patterns published in quilt magazines, and has also been self-publishing for her own company, Needlings, Inc. She has been noted for her 1930's fabric designs for the past fourteen years—first with Chanteclaire Fabrics and more recently with Robert Kaufman Fabrics.

Visit Darlene at www.feedsacklady.com.

PATTERNS AND TEMPLATES

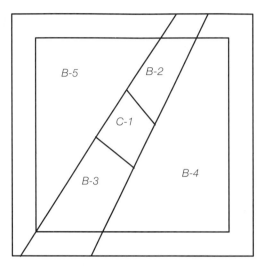

ELEGANCE Cornerstone Pattern
Reproduce at 100%
B=Background fabric
C=Color fabric

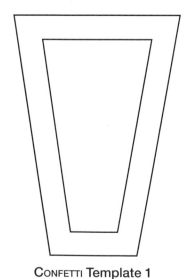

CONFETTI Template 1
Reproduce at 100%

*Add seam allowances
on this edge only.*

CONFETTI Template 2
Reproduce at 100%

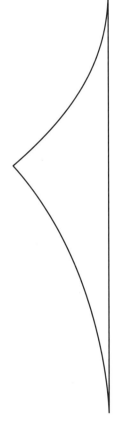

CONFETTI Notch Pattern
Reproduce at 100%

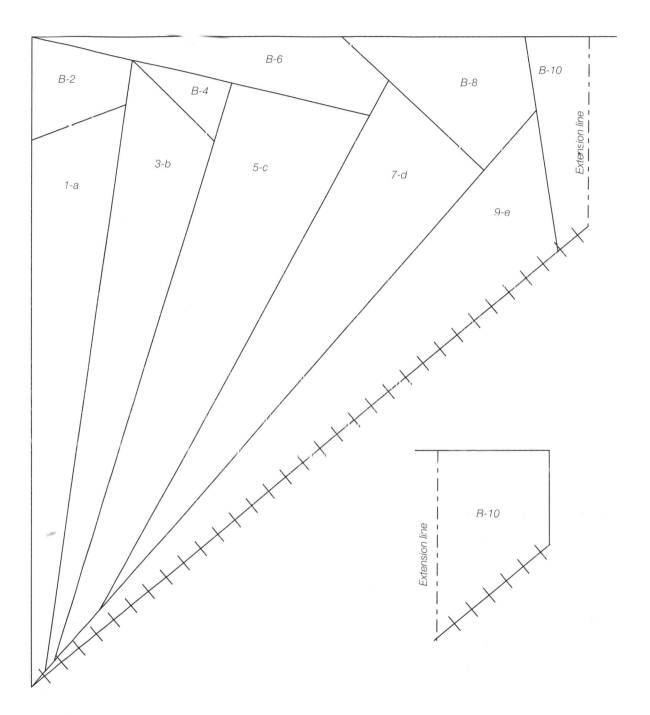

B-2

B-4

B-6

B-8

B-10

1-a

3-b

5-c

7-d

9-e

Extension line

B-10

Extension line

ELEGANCE Big Fan Section

Shown at 75%; Reproduce at 133%

B=Background fabric

Lower case letters indicate different fan fabrics.

Add ¼" seam allowance around the perimeter for the cutting line.

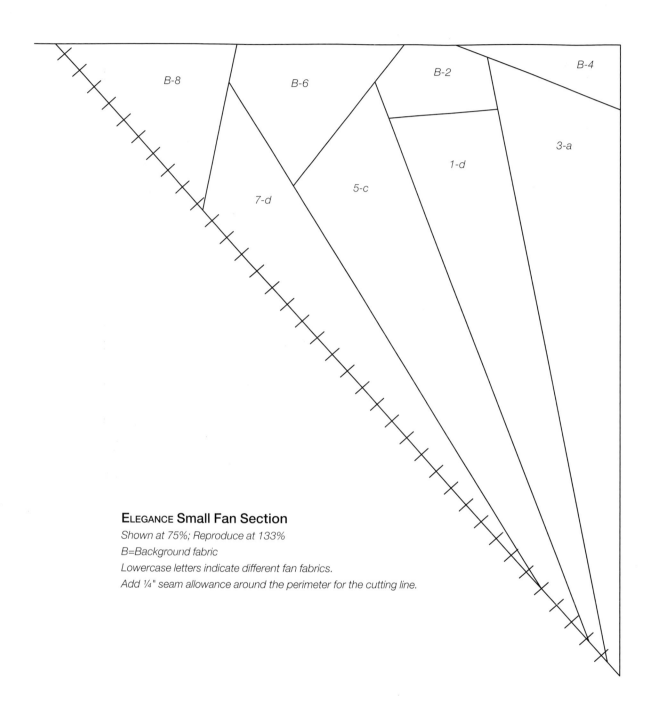

ELEGANCE Small Fan Section
Shown at 75%; Reproduce at 133%
B=Background fabric
Lowercase letters indicate different fan fabrics.
Add ¼" seam allowance around the perimeter for the cutting line.

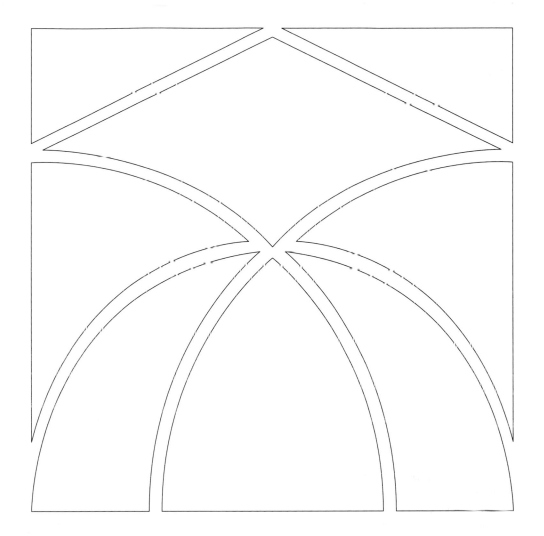

SPINNING WHEEL Pattern

Shown at 50%; Reproduce at 200%

La Bohemia Wall Quilt Pattern (top half)
Reproduce at 100%

LA BOHEMIA WALL QUILT Pattern (bottom half)
Reproduce at 100%

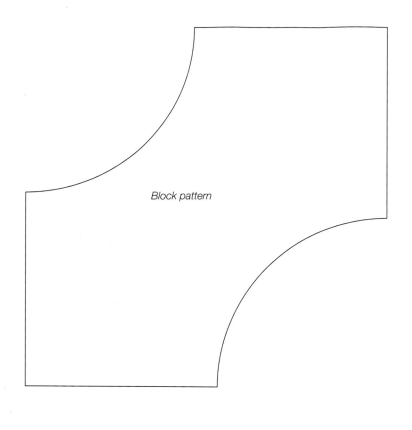

STRIPPIN' IN THE GARDEN Patterns
Shown at 50%; Reproduce at 200%

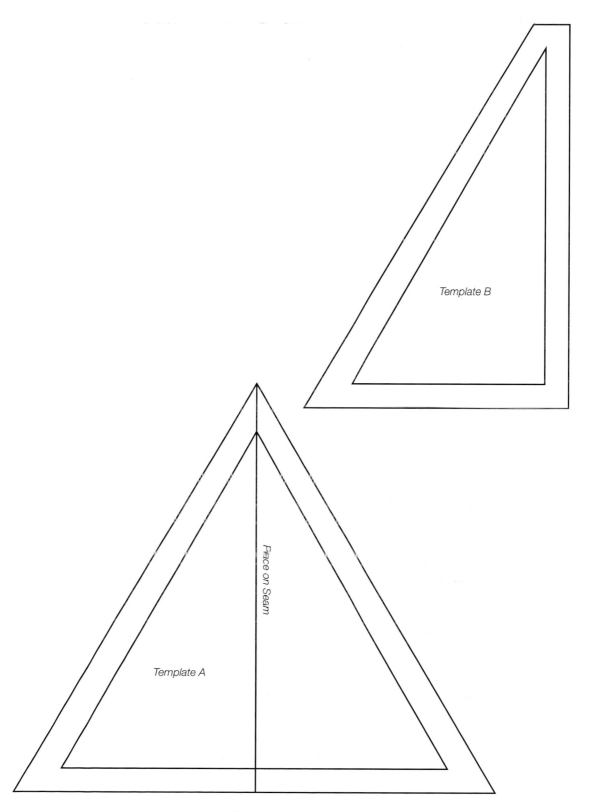

Template B

Face on Seam

Template A

GLOWING STARS Templates
Reproduce at 100%

Sunny Poppy Club Pattern

Shown at 50%; Reproduce at 200%
Photocopy in sections to achieve size, if necessary.

INDEX

MORE SENSATIONAL QUILTING!

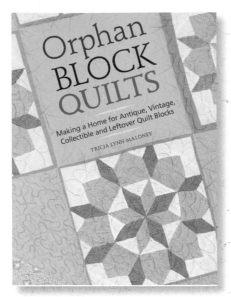

ORPHAN BLOCK QUILTS
Making a Home for Antique, Vintage, Collectible and Leftover Quilt Blocks

Tricia Lynn Maloney

Orphaned blocks can find their way into any quilter's life. Whether they are leftover from an unfinished project, collectible blocks found at a garage sale, or even antique blocks discovered in your great-aunt's attic, Tricia Lynn Maloney will teach you how to care for your orphan blocks, and make a home for them. Whether your orphan blocks are antique, vintage, collectible or simply leftover from a recent project, you can sew the perfect setting that will let the blocks shine!

paperback; 8.25" × 10.875";
128 pages
ISBN-10: 1-4402-0552-3
ISBN-13: 978-1-4402-0552-1
SRN: Z6143

STASH WITH SPLASH QUILTS

Cindy Casciato

All quilters have a fabric stash at home that they don't know how to use. Author Cindy Casciato gives you inspiring quilt patterns, many with size and color variations, to showcase your stash fabrics with a zinger fabric thrown in for splash. You will also learn time-saving techniques, explore new fabric cutting methods, and receive tips and hints from quilting expert Nancy Zieman. An included DVD steps you through a variety of techniques and projects. You'll love the opportunity to use fabrics from your stash while making these gorgeous quilts!

paperback; 8.25" × 10.875";
128 pages + DVD
ISBN-10: 0-89689-811-3
ISBN-13: 978-0-89689-811-0
SRN: Z2918

MAGNIFICENT SPIRAL MANDALA QUILTS

RaNae Merrill

In her follow-up to *Simply Amazing Spiral Quilts*, RaNae Merrill brings you even more spiral possibilities. From bold, kaleidoscopic stars bursting with color to delicate ribbons swirling around a lacy mandala, you can use RaNae's instructions to foundation piece the quilt of your dreams. Whether you simply want to follow one of RaNae's breathtaking quilt patterns, or start from scratch to create your own unique spiral mandala design, this book contains everything you need.

paperback; 8.25" × 10.875";
160 pages
ISBN-10: 1-4402-0425-X
ISBN-13: 978-1-4402-0425-8
SRN: Z5818